Sacred Waters

STORIES OF HEALING, CLEANSING, AND RENEWAL

Maril Crabtree

Author of *Sacred Feathers* and *Sacred Stones*

Adams Media
Avon, Massachusetts

Published by
Adams Media, an F+W Publications Company
57 Littlefield Street, Avon, MA 02322. U.S.A.
www.adamsmedia.com

ISBN: 1-59337-286-8

Printed in Canada.

J I H G F E D C B A

Library of Congress Cataloging-in-Publication Data
Sacred waters / [compiled by] Maril Crabtree.
       p.   cm.
ISBN 1-59337-286-8
1. Water--Meditations. I. Crabtree, Maril.

BL450.S33 2005
202'.12--dc22

2004026918

This book is available at quantity discounts for bulk purchases.
For information, please call 1-800-872-5627.

THIS BOOK IS DEDICATED TO

My husband, Jim, whose love flows like water

~

Contents

PART TWO
WATER MEMORIES: STORIES OF
RECOLLECTION AND REMINISCENCE

~ Contents ~

PART THREE
WATER LEGACIES: STORIES OF
SACRED WATER SITES

PART FOUR
THE MYSTERY OF WATER:
STORIES OF MAGIC AND MYSTERY

Contents

Acknowledgments

I would like to thank my writer friends, especially The Rubber Band Writers Group (Jacqueline Guidry, Sheila Myers, Elizabeth Uppman, and Victoria Williams) and the Kansas City Writers Group, for their ongoing support in helping me be the best writer I can be. Thanks to all the members of my extended family who help me keep the details straight, and straighten out my head when it gets too full to carry more. Thanks to my editors, Kate Epstein and Bridget Brace, who give advice and assistance in a most supportive way.

Introduction

In the world there is nothing more submissive and weak than water. Yet for attacking that which is hard and strong nothing can surpass it.

—LAO-TZU

From the amniotic fluid we swim in before birth, to the cleansing power of waterfalls, rivers, oceans, fountains, and our own tears; from baptismal fonts, to the healing pools of hot springs and natural grottoes; from the sacred waters of Lourdes in France or the Dead Sea in Israel, to the birdbath or swimming pool in your backyard—water contains a unique spiritual energy.

Water can shift from ice to liquid, from snow to steam. It is essential to our survival and covers much of the surface of our planet. Water's power can destroy or give life, can heal our spirits and soothe our bodies, can be a source of great awe, beauty, and inspiration—as well as a source of fear and terror. And our bodies, of course, owe much of their substance to water.

Water connects us to ancient powers existing from the beginning of creation. All cultures throughout time have revered and protected water's life-giving properties. Western myths give us Neptune and Poseidon reigning over the oceans, Venus and Aphrodite rising from the sea, and thousands of nymphs and sprites ruling over rivers, creeks, springs, and fountains. The Japanese brought offerings each year to their rain gods, Kawakami and Kibune. Egyptians worshipped the Nile as a source of fertility and abundance, and believed death involved the soul's journey across another river—the Styx.

On January 1, Brazilians celebrate the festival of Yemanje, an ocean goddess whose origins go back to Africa. In Rio, more than 1 million celebrants dress in white and wade into the ocean at dusk to give homage to her.

These are only a few of the hundreds of deities connected with the recognition of water as a source of spiritual power and as an element basic to our very existence.

In *Sacred Waters* you'll find true stories, meditations, and poems about the power and mystery of water in its many forms. These stories show how water can be a source of guidance and inspiration to illuminate our life journeys—even when it comes in the form of a flood or a near drowning.

You'll learn ways to incorporate the spiritual energies of water through ceremonies and rituals. You'll read about the healing power of oceans, lakes, and hot springs. You'll see how water intersects with human experience in surprising and even mystical ways. These stories show how water's sacred qualities flow through the universe, as a source of life and spiritual wisdom for us all.

Part One

The Power of Water: Stories of Healing and Empowerment

The Sacred Sound of Water

MARIL CRABTREE

What is it about the sound of the ocean? Part of the magic lies in its relentless rhythm, the kind of sound that soothes and perhaps returns us to our prebirth existence, surrounded by the whooshing rhythms of the womb. Whatever the reason, the first time I slept to the sound of the ocean changed my life.

My husband and I, both landlocked Kansans, attended a conference in the Mexican coastal resort town of Puerto Vallarta. When we checked in to our hotel, we found that our room faced the ocean, with only a wall of glass separating us from that vast expanse of water.

That night, I slid open the glass doors and heard the sound of ocean waves caressing the shore. The room was dark except for starlight. As I climbed into bed and closed my eyes, I pictured myself on a little boat being carried across the sky, as in the nursery rhyme "Wynken, Blinken, and Nod," propelled by the sound of rolling waves directly below my window.

In five minutes I was sound asleep, but I awoke several times that first night simply to listen to that infinite sacred sound, to marvel at the ocean's timeless presence. I understood for the first time why people choose to live by the sea.

Over the next few years, I made trip after trip to beach areas in Hawaii, California, Florida, and Maine.

I didn't care if I could *see* the ocean from my room; I only wanted to hear it as I slept. That lullaby of waves filled my soul.

I continue to love ocean sounds. I've expanded my embrace to include the sounds of waterfalls trickling down hillsides on Maui's road to Hana, or roaring down cliffs in the Colorado Rockies; the whooshing sounds of geysers erupting in Yellowstone National Park; the almost silent sound of underground pools making their way through the depths; the whisper of creeks and rivers meandering through mountain meadows.

When I'm near the sound of water, I always pause and give thanks for something that calls me to a sacred sense of self, something that creates a connection with all of life.

Spirit of the Water

Patricia Wellingham-Jones

I wake to your voice.
No other place on the planet
holds my heart.
I have no wish to leave your side.
You've spoiled me.

You bounce children's laughter
on tubes in spring
bathe my limbs in summer.

My eyes rest on your steady flow
on salmon churning upstream in autumn
on winter crash of flood.

You teach me to slow my heart
to rhythms of the land
its steadying bass voice
throbs under human rushing.

The riffle of your tongue
soothes a brain fevered with excess.

I live beside your musical journey
as you slide from Mount Lassen
to the river, to the sea.

Let me listen every waking sleeping hour.
I do not wish to impose
my voice on yours
o spirit of the water.

Surrender

SHELLEY ANN WAKE

I walked along the break wall five paces behind my family as the usual thoughts ran through my head. *You don't fit in. You're not good enough. You'll never be enough.*

The rest of my family mingled and chatted. They didn't seem to miss me. Families coming the other way laughed their way around me. I put my arms to my sides to let them pass, frowning at the thought that I was always just a person in the way.

Young girls in swimsuits wandered calmly past. I wondered how they managed to feel so free. I couldn't even wear a swimsuit on the beach. How could they walk around in one so happily?

I was fourteen. I was supposed to be young and free like those girls. Why was I walking alone feeling so sad? Why wasn't I smiling and laughing? Everything around me seemed to taunt me, as it always did. Happy family, happy young girls, happy world, and then me.

I walked a few more steps behind, partly because I wanted to blend in to nothingness and partly because I thought walking sadly alone might be my destiny. Then my family stopped walking and stood staring out to sea. I stopped a few steps behind them and looked out. The first thing I noticed was the people standing on the island opposite.

Everyone's eyes seemed to be fixed on the same point. Some people were completely still, some were waving their arms around, and one woman was crouching down with her head in her hands.

Then I saw what they were staring at. A boat had overturned halfway between the island and the break wall. The boat was on its side and floating in the choppy sea. As the boat floated away, I saw what the people were so concerned about. A man was splashing around in the water. He was in the deep ocean, far from the island, far from the shore, and was being slowly pushed farther out to sea.

I watched as he attempted to swim back toward the island. Even as he did so, the current pushed him farther out. His strokes became more frantic as he struggled against the current. His arms waved wildly in a final attempt to swim. His panicked movements did nothing, with his arms hardly touching the water. Still, he continued.

He began to sink beneath the water. He was gone for a minute and then he emerged, still waving his arms around trying to propel himself back toward the shore. I could see rescue boats on their way to him now. But he didn't see them or hear them. People on the break wall started yelling, pointing toward the rescue boats coming from several directions. The man turned in wild circles, as if he thought the pointing was telling him which way to go. Or maybe he thought the people were pointing out sharks. He turned in frantic circles, going under and then reappearing again.

I stood back and watched the scene. As the man turned in circles, I couldn't help but think that there was a message here for me. Here was this man who was going to drown because he couldn't calm down and wait to be saved. He had to splish and splash and try to save himself. He had to fight the ocean when the ocean could not be beaten. I could see that all he had to do was stop fighting and he would be all right.

"Surrender," I suddenly screamed. "Just surrender and you'll float."

I don't think he actually heard me, but suddenly that's just what he did. In the middle of the ocean, on this choppy sea, he suddenly stopped struggling and just floated. His body moved calmly up as the waves passed under him, and then calmly down again as the waves moved out to sea. He lay on top of this moving ocean and let it move him as it pleased. A few minutes later, the rescue boats arrived and he was saved.

My family stood shaking their heads for a little while. Then they started walking again. I didn't move. I stood staring out to sea, thinking about how that man had almost drowned, when saving himself seemed so easy from where I was standing. Yet from his spot in the water, it wouldn't have seemed so easy.

The usual thoughts ran through my head. *You're not good enough, not fun enough, not pretty enough, not loved enough.* Then that one word returned to me: *surrender.* I thought about my insecurities and how I was always sad that I could never escape from them. I thought about how I felt weaker because I could never beat them.

Surrender, I whispered to myself.

The thoughts and insecurities did not disappear in a heartbeat, but I did surrender to them. I stopped struggling against them and floated above them, letting the tide of thoughts drift past me.

I turned and looked at my family, walking far ahead of me now. Then I ran. I ran down that break wall, blended into my family, and walked with them. I let the thoughts flow under me, and as I found myself involved in conversation, I began to feel content.

On that day, I became a person floating on the sea, and I remain one. My life has not always been smooth. I've had my share of choppiness, but I always float with the tide and I have never been pulled under. On that day, the sea taught me to surrender.

There's Something About an Island

MARCIA FAIRBANKS

"Have you looked at a globe lately?" a friend asked, when I began to wax lyrical about places I have loved the best. "We all live on islands," she smirked.

I meant a limited piece of geography surrounded by water, unattached to the mainland by bridge or causeway. I retreated from my friend's scoffing, raised my drawbridge, and islanded myself.

I wasn't born an island girl, but the sea has always been with me. I lived a short walk down a dirt road from a Cape Cod beach when I was a child. I stood at a place called White Cliffs holding my dad's hand when hurricanes' waves crashed against the rocks below. I sat on a sea wall and gazed across the water toward Portugal whenever the blues threatened to overtake me. The foreverness of the tide, leaving but always returning.

The smells of salt-crusted shells. Sun-baked sand. Kelp and Irish moss fermenting on the shore. Low-tide muck. The scent of *Rosa rugosa* with its velveteen petals and vicious thorns. The feel of sticky gray clay beneath the beach sand if I dug deep enough. Where do the stars go when the sun shines? Look, they dance on the surface of the sea. Wharves, piers, jetties, and boardwalks over marshland were the playgrounds of my youth.

I believe in the ion theory of sea air. Negative ions wafting off the ocean interact with the outer layers of our cells, altering our brain chemistry.

I seek every opportunity to take that giant step from the mainland to islands, where there are fewer worldly distractions. Where I can quietly come to conclusions, about a few things at least. Yet, I must make an effort to get there. I must travel light, select my essentials carefully.

Then, the last transport off-island departs and I am marooned. At the mercy of weather—sun or fog, wind and rain—more intense because there is no escape. And the natives might not be friendly.

Islanders tend to distrust, perhaps even dislike, outsiders. I approach the locals as I would a strange dog. Stand still, let them sniff, extend a hand cautiously. Smile, but do not stare. Listen more than talk; when I do talk, speak softly. I respect their property rights. Space is finite in their world.

I have, from early childhood, been entranced by maps of real or imaginary places: Tolkien's Middle Earth, Faulkner's Yoknapatawpha County, and especially the elegant cartography in moldy atlases where sea serpents rule. I snatch up maps of a chosen island as soon as I step off the boat. I like the ones that look hand-drawn by a ten-year-old adventure seeker. Place names like Copicut Neck, Plover Hill, Smutty Nose, and the inevitable Deadman's Cove lure me on. I carry one map in my back pocket, keep another in my backpack. Each night before sleep, I mark with a pink felt pen my day's journey around the fragile border between land and water, the better to reinforce memory and pleasant dreams.

The contradictions of an island fascinate me. Encapsulated life, cut off from the mainland by weather or calamity, nevertheless grants a sense of safety and security from the bad things loose in the outside world. I once read comments by an island's residents about where they vacation when they need to "get off the rock." They go to other islands.

"I just came back from a trip to the mainland," one said. "I don't like it out there."

Insular. Inaccessible. Self-contained. Finite. But with a limitless view. Islands are simple, straightforward places where pretensions are difficult to maintain, but eccentricity is easy. I appreciate the challenges islanders face and wish I were truly one of them.

I go to my islands often—in times of love and strife. There I feel cupped in the center of creation. Waves of infinite possibility undulate in every direction—dissolution, union, transformation. Surrounded by the sea, I am, once again, newborn.

Unseen Currents

VIRGINIA FORTNER

I haven't always loved water. Growing up on a farm, my evening chore was to lower a bucket far down into the cistern, haul it up hand-over-hand, and carry water to contrary animals. The geese hissed at me, the chickens walked through the trough with dirty feet, one goat tried to butt the pail before I emptied it, and the pigs rooted until their trough overturned in mud.

My first images of water were associated with danger and judgment. Things I *should* and *should not* do surrounded me often, like Psalm 93's "mighty waves of the sea." *Wash behind your ears. Do the dishes without being told. Don't go too close to the pond. Watch for snakes near the river.*

Childhood nightmares brought walls of water rushing, ready to swallow me. I took swimming lessons in the hometown pool. As I practiced a few times in the presence of family at a local swimming hole—a pond shared with cattle—I always kept my head above the murky, smelly depths through which I thrashed. Over the years, my swimming capability grew as I spent time in clean city pools.

Fully grown and on my first solo trip to Hawaii, I found delight in surrendering myself to the ocean's friendly rhythms. Poseidon himself seemed to stir up sand with incoming waves, sending them forth to a calm horizon with a lift of his trident. I floated, sidestroked, and tumbled like a happy sea creature.

One sunny afternoon, I swam with a native friend and her daughter. We swam far out past the breaking waves before we turned back toward the beach. Soon, they were walking out of the water, but I was still far from shore. I doubled my efforts to reach them. Instead of moving toward the strip of sand, I was carried farther away from it. Every muscle ached. I felt I could not lift my arms again. With the little breath I had left, I called out. I doubted anyone could hear me.

It seemed like an eternity passed. I knew I floated away at the mercy of the sea. I closed my eyes and heard a deep voice say, "Need a little help?"

Two blond surfers pulled me across a surfboard, where I lay too exhausted to even hold on properly. They towed me to where my feet felt blessed sand. When my strength returned, so did the terror and resignation I had felt in the water's power.

After reading about the proper way to swim in an undertow, I was surprised to feel drawn back to that spot. No friends were with me, but the beach was full of people. Some swam beyond the breakers, seeming at ease in the sparkling water.

Fear momentarily clutched at my thinking. What if that same shifting sand was at work under the inviting surface? I could actually drown this time. The weakness I had felt in those waters, when I gave up the struggle that first time, gave way to a different kind of acceptance.

I decided that, if it was my time to leave this earth, this was a powerful, beautiful place for it to happen. I felt wise and strong. Any fear that was left felt healthy, melting into a kind of curiosity. Could I actually swim with an unseen current and find myself nearer my destination? I waded a while, then swam cautiously beyond the first wave. It felt wonderful. Adrenalin flowed, and I ventured a little farther, feeling vigilant, but brave. Finally, beyond the breakers, I floated and swam without any tidal tugs that day.

Driving back to that Oahu beach years later, I saw that it foreshadowed situations in my life. Time and events unexpectedly changed my course, often without my having control—job loss, divorce, moves I hadn't dreamed would happen.

When major changes come, my initial reaction is often still panic. Then my fear gives over to a curious need to observe what happens next. I set my intention to learn the lesson needed, and the results invariably turn out easier or better than I expected.

Now, having felt the buoyancy and tasted the salty tang of four oceans, I'm still waiting for Poseidon to carry me forth so I can try to swim with, not against, the strength of unseen currents. In life, I've found that becoming part of unseen spiritual currents is what thrills my soul and brings unexpected joy.

Daily Respite

LISA WATERMAN GRAY

I didn't know how much I wanted one until "my" fountain appeared on the shelf of a nature store in the mall. As I looked at it, I felt an instantaneous longing to take it home. A high-gloss, midnight black ceramic bowl cradled hefty, jagged layers of charcoal-colored slate, topped with a four-inch-long vase that gently poured water across the slate landscape. My shoulders relaxed, and I visualized a tiny mountain stream trickling over pebbles.

I checked the price and gasped. Much as I wanted the fountain, I knew that buying it would seriously pinch my pocketbook. I left empty-handed and told myself that, if the fountain remained on its shelf the next time I visited, I could have it.

I returned to the nature store several weeks before Christmas. The unmistakable music of water crossing slate drew me forward and my breath slowed. Nevertheless, for some reason, I couldn't bring myself to purchase the fountain. As I left the store, a sign in the front window caught my attention—"Holiday sale. 20% off all items." The sale ended at the close of the business day.

I suddenly knew what to do. Christmas was fast approaching, with my birthday only a couple of months later. As soon as I entered the house, I sought out my husband. Rarely had I so pointedly asked for a specific gift.

"Mark, I know what I want for Christmas—and my birthday, if necessary. There's this fountain at the nature store in the mall that I'm absolutely nuts about. I've already looked at it twice. It's twenty percent off through the end of today. So, if you have any interest at all in getting it for me, you need to go over there before they close."

Mark nodded and returned to his garage workshop. Several hours later, he left to run an errand. He returned with a large box on which the word "fountain" was printed. My heart raced.

"Merry Christmas," Mark said.

"Should I wait to open it?"

"No, don't wait. You already know what it is, so you might as well enjoy it now."

"Thank you, hon'. I really, really love it." I hugged him hard and kissed his cheek.

Within an hour, I had assembled the fountain and found a spot for it beside my favorite living room chair.

Within a day, the melody of trickling water on slate added images of the natural world to my daily meditations.

Within a week, I couldn't imagine walking through the house without hearing the fountain's music. Even as I worked in my upstairs office I kept it turned on so that, when I checked the mail or the refrigerator, I would be aware of the fountain's calming presence.

For several years I basked in the soothing natural sound every day, babied the tiny motor with distilled water refills, and gingerly cleaned every piece of the fountain whenever the motor rasped with effort.

When a gangly puppy joined our family last spring, another use for the fountain emerged. One morning a lapping sound accompanied the fountain's gentle music. With his feet perched precariously at table's edge, Petey drank in measured strokes. As the weeks progressed, Petey's lapping turned to gulps and I purchased a second bottle of distilled water each week.

A year later, Petey still drinks from the fountain and I still meditate at the water's edge each morning. On the rare occasions when I forget to start the fountain, or have turned it off until I find time to clean it properly, the house seems empty—even with the droning TV, the onslaught of incoming evening phone calls for my teenage daughter, and Petey's protective bark as he gazes out the window.

In the midst of modern life's noise, the fountain reminds me of all the rushing rivers, pounding breakers, and gentle rainstorms I have experienced, re-creating timeless natural beauty in my living room every day.

Transformation

BILL GROVER

For much of my life, water has been nearby—lakes in Michigan, the inlet by Anchorage, the Pacific off Newport Beach and the Bay Area, and, for the last twenty-five years, the Gulf of Mexico.

Reserving a time to swim with dolphins in the Florida Keys, though, was completely outside my routine. On a warm winter afternoon in January, my friend and I joined seven other men, women, and children in Key Largo for an orientation.

During our meeting, we learned that the inlet where we would swim was home to five dolphins. Jason, our leader, asked us to respect that, and to let them make the first contact.

"Dolphins typically find men less interesting than women and children," Jason warned.

I understood the social protocol, and could hear the expectation of disappointment bouncing through my mind.

A few yards away, the five dolphins frolicked and raced, making huge splashes when they broke the surface and dived into the air. We could hear their squeals.

"Sounds like they're looking forward to meeting you," Jason grinned.

The children were curious, present, innocent, ready, spontaneous. Considering how out of touch with my emotions I was, it is surprising that my excitement seeped through. I didn't notice my attitude any more than I was aware I was breathing air.

Each of us selected fins and a mask. We plunged into the vast inlet, treading water and waiting for our dolphin friends to make contact. I heard the delighted laughter and yelling of children when dolphins came close on a slow swim-by. They swam with grace and agility, even though they were at least six feet long.

They swam by fast and slow, breathing air and diving again, behaving like kids on a playground. We heard their sonar clicking everywhere, as the energy waves reflected off our bodies. In these few minutes, we allowed them to explore and know us, their senses revealing whether we were safe and if we were interesting enough to play with.

I wasn't aware of being dissatisfied until midway through our time. I heard laughter coming from the children and women around me. Our graceful playmates were touching and being touched, and were generally interacting with most of us. I wasn't having any action at all.

At some point, the little kid in me got frustrated. The voices in my head said that there was something about me, or what I was or wasn't doing in the water, that was lacking. My excitement was going to be wasted. My fellow adventurers were having all the fun.

Looking for something to do, like a consolation prize, I reached for a small rubber ball floating nearby. I began to amuse and content myself, expecting nothing much would happen. That's what loners do.

I wasn't prepared when a dolphin surfaced unexpectedly in front of me, bottle-nosed mouth wide open. We were a couple of feet apart. Her huge body was right next to me. Jason yelled over that she was Toni and she loved to play. She eyed the ball, and I imagined her sounds said, "Can I play?"

OK, let's play, here's the ball, I thought, and tossed it to Toni.

She grabbed it on the fly, and submerged. Tilting my mask forward into the water, I looked beneath the surface as she released and caught it underwater, like a pooch playing with a ball.

The ball quickly floated to the surface when Toni dropped it. I snatched it up, and she was beside me clicking her playful requests and waiting. I varied our game and threw it higher with the same result. Toni was great at playing catch.

I pulled the ball underwater and passed it off. In search of something to keep her around, I swam in a circle and held the ball out for Toni. That worked. I rotated faster so that the play and tease had her following the ball, trying to catch up like a kitten chasing a string.

I'd lost track of time and place. We were alone in the water, just Toni and me. A second dolphin surfaced.

"That's Roscoe," shouted Jason. "He wants to play, too."

Roscoe joined in the game. I was overwhelmed and playing like I was twelve again. A couple of minutes later, Emily joined us. I was swimming with the "in" crowd. They were vying for the ball above and below. They were everywhere, brushing against me. Now I was eight again!

The whistle shrilled, calling us to get out of the water. Our time was up. I couldn't have been more like a resentful kid on a warm summer's evening, tirelessly playing outside with best friends, when your parents make you go in because it's getting late. "Time for bed. You've had a big day."

I hung back in the water as long as I could, wondering how I could stay and have some fun, have something happen that would erase the disappointment, a least a little.

Like those summer evenings long ago, I had no choice. I caught up with the others as they took off the swim gear and handed it in, thanking our hosts.

My friend and I walked away from the water and headed toward our car. So, it was over. I had been right about being disappointed.

She intruded into my upset with her observations. "You were really having a good time out there." I looked at her with disbelief, and thought, *What is she talking about? I hardly had any fun at all!*

"What do you mean?" I said.

"Well, there were two or three dolphins swimming with you for quite a while," she said. "They picked you to play ball with, and the rest of us mostly watched you, and wondered how you could pull off something like that."

I was confused. First I thought, *She's right, they were with me, but it wasn't any fun.* I was beginning to hear my other thoughts, though: *Wait a minute, maybe she's right, maybe I was having a good time.*

I listened to the internal confusion. In the next moment, it was as if I were watching a movie in my head, replaying the scene with Toni, Roscoe, and Emily. All of that "no fun" exploded into a spectacular blast of excitement as I realized that I had, indeed, captured the attention of three dolphins.

The part of me that was watching the fast replay movie was simultaneously aware that I had had two completely real experiences: "This is no fun, I'm disappointed"

and "That was off the map, I had a great time." I understand how two people sitting in the same movie interpret
scenes or characters or even the whole movie differently,
but here, I had the ability to be joyful and resentful at the
same moment, depending on where I stood to interpret
my experience.

I saw that my experience depended on my own
choices. What if the simple pure play of life in the present
moment was getting constantly filtered through a mask
of *something is missing, this isn't it?* What if I was actually
having the time of my life and didn't know it, wouldn't let
myself know it, and instead was spending my life trying
(unsuccessfully) to find what I always had?

The light of understanding flooded me as if I had
once again plunged into that inlet. I understood at last
that, there in the water, I had a sacred, life-expanding,
soul-connecting transformation of my experience.

I realized that I had an expectation and attitude
about life that made sure I had no fun, no matter what. I
saw that I had a choice to reinterpret my experience by
putting myself in the present, without the constant nag-
ging of my "inner critic," who was out to prove that life
would disappoint me.

To this day, I cherish the insights that unfolded from
my sacred water experience with the dolphins.

Immersing a Sand-Coated Hand in Water

-FOR DAVE LAUER

KARL ELDER

Done with all that fuss at the office,
here with the kids, back of the house,
kneeling before a bucket by a big old tire,
glove of grit to the wrist.
How could anyone earn this moment—
like swirls of flesh unfurling
soon as my hand is under,
how it would have to look,
feel,
entering the afterlife:
the spirit smoldering,
quenched.

Fresh Water for Robins

PEGGY EASTMAN

Be praised, my Lord, through our sister water,
So helpful and so unpretentious, precious and simple.

—ST. FRANCIS, "CANTICLE OF THE SUN"

I had dug a small depression in the middle of my backyard garden and placed the cast cement statue of St. Francis there for birds on the wing, a marker so they could find their way to the birdbath nearby.

I felt certain this statue would draw them to the fresh water I put out for them, just as birds had been drawn to the real St. Francis. Wasn't he often pictured with arms outstretched, birds perched on his shoulders?

When I looked at the statue's calm face, I felt tranquil, too. How had the sculptor been able to capture so much serenity? The birds coming for fresh water sometimes perched on the statue's head; I doubted that the real St. Francis would have minded.

But this day had not gone well, and I couldn't seem to provide any discipline to my scattered activities or feel any peace. Where to start? What to do first? Anxiously, I chewed on a wooden pencil, which bore tooth marks from previous chewings. I felt so full of worry, so inadequate. Yet, what was all this worry accomplishing? I hadn't even opened the door and stepped outside to smell the air or see the leaves beginning to feather the tree branches.

Walking from the living room into my kitchen to run water for dirty dishes, I looked out the back window and saw them: seven robins ringing my birdbath. Robins, the first sign of spring—*this* spring. They were unmistakably robins, their chests orange-red, their backs and wings dark gray, their slim pointed beaks yellow as corn. The robins were trying to get some drinking water from my birdbath with those sharp beaks, tipping their heads back to let the liquid slide down. But the bottom of the birdbath was sludgy. I hadn't yet given it a spring scrubbing, and what water was there was darkened by the tannic acid of withered winter leaves.

The robins twittered in a flute-like bird chorus that might have come from seven small wind instruments. The chorus was prolonged and persistent, as if the robins were performing a rite sacred to them. Perhaps it was.

With no warning, tears filled my eyes. Taxes. Bills. House dust. What did it all matter, really? What could it matter compared to what robins needed to do to survive in the wild? These robins had flown hundreds of miles, perhaps thousands, to winter down south. Now, with the ice thawing up north, they were on their way, migratory travelers reenacting their ancient ritual of spring. They were welcome visitors pausing for refreshment, as human wayfarers in ancient times might have paused in a village and asked a stranger for a drink of water.

All they asked, these feathered visitors, was a fresh drink of water. Just a simple drink of clear, clean water. I went to find the bristly yellow scrub-brush I used to clean my birdbath.

The birds would continue on their way north until they found their place of temporary rest, where the females would build their mud-walled nests.

All the robins wanted was clean water for the journey. Robins couldn't turn on a spigot, as I could. I reached for my jacket.

The robins at the birdbath twittered more cheerily, seemingly glad for a resting place. As I watched, one robin flew up onto the statue's head. All they asked for was fresh water, and I hadn't even scrubbed out the birdbath and filled it for them. How many times had the real St. Francis cleaned and filled a birdbath? How many times had he risen early to pray and work, listening to the calls of birds who brought the lightening sky of dawn with their wings?

I went to the basement door to unlock it.

The robins seemed to have no doubts that their days would be good. The mother robin would scout earthworms for her skinny, open-mouthed, squawking babies when the turquoise blue eggs hatched, plucking the plump worms out of the ground after a spring rain with her probing yellow beak.

When the fledgling young developed feathers, they would be ready to try flight, and the father robin would appear to oversee their first awkward attempts. The father robin would have to protect his unwary fledglings from diving hawks and domestic predators: stalking cats and sniffing dogs off the leash. To reach adulthood is a feat for a baby robin. But the parent robins did not dwell on the dangers around them.

I filled a bucket with clear, cool water in my basement laundry room.

So many miles of flying. So much feathered work. So much effort for such a small bird. So much to do to try to ensure survival in a world made more hostile by the threats of tract-house overbuilding and once-domestic cats gone wild.

I looked out the glass panes of the basement door. The robin that had flown onto the head of St. Francis flew back onto the birdbath, alighting on the rim as if signaling for water. As I watched the seven robins sitting on the edge of my birdbath, proudly erect, sending their persistent chorus into the shadow-lengthening hours of the waning day, I felt a deep sense of gratitude for their presence. The gratitude quieted my anxious spirit.

Robins didn't feel inadequate, so why should I? Robins didn't worry, so why should I? How did they know there would be fresh water to drink on their long, seasonal treks south and north? How did they know the ground would be moist enough for earthworms? How did they know there would be berries to eat?

The gratitude I felt changed to a sense of urgency. Water. I must give these feathered messengers water. Now. I did not think of the other work left to do. I did not think of taxes or dust or bills to pay. I did not think of anything but opening the door to scrub out my birdbath and fill it with fresh, clean water.

At my approach, the robins flew into the bushes. They seemed to be watching, for when I had scrubbed out the birdbath, filled it with clean water, and retreated into the basement, they returned to drink. Now more robins flew in to drink, as if some robin signal had been sent on the air: *fresh water here.* Several robins immersed themselves, then fluffed their feathers while resting on the concrete rim.

After the robins had finished drinking and had flown off, I filled the birdbath again and sat on the curved stone bench by the garden. I felt the touch of afternoon sun on my face. I saw the green of newly unfurling leaves—the color of baby asparagus—as they shivered in a light breeze that still had a touch of winter about its edges.

This time of peace and gratitude was my gift from the returning robins, who asked only for a drink of fresh water to help them complete the ancient rite of their journey north.

Mosquito Breath and the Song of the Creek

Virginia Lore

What I remember most about that time in my life is how I woke up every day in pain. I tried to make a joke out of it. People asked what I did at parties and I said, "I live in perpetual anguish."

Not only was I given to panic attacks and depression, but I also had the habit of trying to address my angst by hurting myself. I was twenty-two, living in an apartment complex for mentally ill adults, and trying to outgrow the beehive of twisted beliefs that led me to cut myself open over and over again.

I knew it wouldn't be like this forever. I knew that hurting myself wouldn't accomplish anything. I was trying to grow spiritually. I worked on lucid dreaming and tried to vaporize clouds. I tried to join the Catholic Church, then threw them over for goddess worship. But as much as I believed things might change in some abstract future, I lived in a cloud of darkness, often crouched on my kitchen floor with a razor blade in my hand, trying to decide whether or not to cut.

One night I tried a new meditation: I tried to imagine a small speck of love within myself, and concentrated on it, allowing it to grow bigger into a large cloud of rose-colored light. I let my image of that love fill me and grow past my skin. I felt it fill my apartment, and grow beyond the roof, encapsulating the city. I saw it stretch out—offering love outward to whoever might need it.

A car horn blared outside and I looked at the clock and realized it was time to watch my favorite cop show, so I abruptly left my image where it was. I hurried to turn on the TV and packed my suitcase while I was watching—my parents would be picking me up in the morning to go on vacation with them.

In the morning, a caravan of cars pulled up outside my apartment complex. Some friends of the family had decided to celebrate their anniversary by sponsoring a retreat in Colorado for whoever wanted to come with them. Free vacation? Right on! I waved to some of the people I knew and joined my parents in their car. As we pulled away from where I lived, I felt an almost instant sense of expectation, a kind of hope I hadn't felt since high school. I knew this was going to be a special week— I just didn't know how special.

The second day we were in Colorado, everyone decided to go into town for miniature golfing. I decided to stay back at the lodge and read, but for some reason I couldn't settle down to my book. The scent of pine and the sound of a rushing creek lured me outdoors, and I began to walk. I had no idea where I was going. I found myself on a trail that went through the woods and just kept walking, putting one foot in front of the other as if in a dream.

After what seemed like an hour, the altitude began to get to me. I could feel every heartbeat, and I felt sick and dizzy. I realized that I hadn't seen anybody on my walk and I started hyperventilating. It occurred to me that I could pass out or die of a heart attack or something and nobody would be around to help me. I started to panic as I rounded a corner, but then I saw it: a slab of stone sitting by the bend of the creek.

It was large and gray, placed next to the path, and the perfect height for sitting on. Something about the place calmed me. The babble of the creek flowing next to me helped me slow my breathing down. I wasn't going to die. A gentle breeze caressed my skin, and I began to feel a sense of peace creeping over me as I listened to the rushing water. I watched the aspen leaves quiver and the ants crawl about my feet.

After a time, a mosquito buzzed around my ear, and without much thought I invited it to land on my arm. I wondered whimsically if God would take the form of a mosquito, when there it was: a cloud of love sent forth in a meditation two days earlier, hovering around me in rosy hue. I realized that the cloud was my own love for myself.

I sat for a while longer, trying to absorb as much of the moment's energy as I could. I imagined the energy of the creek infusing my body, joining me with all of life. I noted with awe that the mosquito bite did not itch.

I sat until the humming of insects started annoying me again, until I could feel the prickle of sweat at my hairline, and I knew it was time to go back. As I emerged from the woods I scribbled some lines down on paper. They became the chorus of a song I wrote that day:

> I wish for you Peace on the other side;
> I wish for you Love along the way;
> I hope you find the Power that makes it all worthwhile;
> I hope you find the Strength to live today.

I'm not sure exactly what happened to me out there by that creek, but I know I was different afterward. Eventually I grew up, stopped hurting myself, and traveled out into the world with a sense of self worth. I finished college, got a job I liked, met my life partner, and had children.

And every once in a while, when the children overwhelm me or my responsibilities seem like too much, I remember that moment in the forest. I whisper the words that bring it all back—"mosquito breath and the song of the creek"—and I feel a lift of grace. Mosquito breath and song of the creek. It's all going to be OK.

A Taste of Freedom

BETTY VIAMONTES

Water, clear water that comes and goes in a gentle motion as I walk barefoot along the edge of Santa Maria Beach, Cuba. I am fifteen. My feet are white and small, and the water covers them as I walk. When the water returns to the sea, the sun shines on my feet, and they glow like the moon.

No glow in the eyes of the people who died at sea. I sit on the sand and think about them. Why did they leave Havana? Why did they risk their lives for freedom when there is no freedom when you die? Or is there? I miss them: Antonio, Maria, their baby Lucia. I even miss the ones I didn't know. They died at sea. The sea was their savior and their executioner.

I get up and walk again. This time, the water reaches my ankles. I look in the distance. Somewhere on another beach up Havana's coast, where Cubans are not allowed, tourists stay in hotels that are only for them, walk on beaches that are not for me. Perhaps that's why Antonio and Maria left with their baby Lucia. They wanted to go wherever they wished and live how the tourists lived. They wanted Lucia to grow up free.

Maybe if I go deeper into the ocean, I will know what it's like to be free. I walk into the water until I can walk no more, until the voices of the children playing on the sand seem distant. When the waves come, they cover me and I hold my breath. Then I watch for the waves and jump. I laugh as I play with the waves. Perhaps this is how freedom feels. It's like the ocean caressing your body and making it silky and clean. It's like the ocean on a sunny afternoon on Santa Maria Beach.

Suddenly, after one of my jumps, I fall deep down into a crevice on the ocean floor. My feet cannot touch bottom. I extend my arms and feel sand at my fingertips, sand that touches my fingers but not my feet. I no longer hear the voices of the children. I only hear the sound of water. I am inside a deep hole in the ocean and no one can see me. *Will I drown?*

Perhaps that is why Antonio and Maria left with their baby. Perhaps they tasted freedom once, and when they lost it, they felt like they were drowning. They were willing to risk their lives to be able to swim in free waters again. Am I willing to die for freedom? It would be so easy.

I think about Mamá, my brother, and my sister. No, I must not surrender to the sea because there is *no* freedom when you die. I panic and swim up as hard as I can. I am afraid. I am trying to hold my breath, but it is increasingly difficult. *Am I going to die?*

I swim and thrust my body upwards, up toward the sky, up until I don't touch sand. At last, I lift my head out of the water and gasp for air. I swim sideways and hear the voices of the children on the beach.

I swim toward the voices.

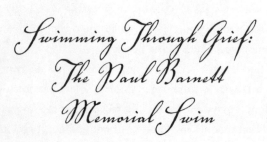

Swimming Through Grief: The Paul Barnett Memorial Swim

Deborah Shouse

In one of my baby pictures, I am standing on a New Hampshire beach, my plump feet in the water, my father kneeling in the sand behind me, smiling proudly. My father loved swimming and he loved it when my brother and I were in the water. Our summer vacations centered around pools, lakes, and oceans. Getting in the water was a great way to connect with, play with, and please my father.

After my father died, I wondered how I could honor him and keep his spirit close to me. It seemed natural to get into my health club pool and start swimming my way through the grieving process. Thus began the Paul Barnett Memorial Swim.

The pool offered two ways of communing. In the crawl stroke, face down, feet concentrated and straight, I was surrounded by the water without being distracted by other swimmers. The back crawl, face out of the water, legs a little more relaxed, gave me a chance to talk out loud to my father. I pulled my arms backwards, and with each stroke I spoke to my Dad.

"I miss you," I said, and tears leaked from my eyes. "I'm so sad that you're no longer here." I felt the emotional tightness of the past three weeks lift as sobs jerked through me. Though I was in the middle lane, no one could see or notice my grief. I felt the luxury of being anonymous and yet of not having to hide my sorrow. I was wet all over, my face awash with both tears and pool water.

As I swam, I thought of the different waters I had been in with Dad—in the early days, when we went to visit our Boston relatives, Dad would stride right into the Atlantic no matter how frigid the temperature. No matter how numb my legs got, how blue my arms, I followed him. Other summers, we ventured to see my mother's family in Miami. Dad spent hours showing us how to body surf, teaching us to love the push and tug of the waves, showing us how to swim in the boisterous sea.

Some summers we stayed home and went to lakes and swimming pools. At the pools, my brother and I always raced Dad, trying to see if we were getting faster. Summer after summer, Dad's crawl stroke beat us. Until age seventeen, when I touched the side of the pool ahead of my father. My triumph was bittersweet—there was a sense of security in being not quite as good as my Dad.

Even after we were scattered and grown, and had our own children, water played a part in our reunions and get-togethers.

"What's the pool like?" was the first question Dad asked about a potential gathering spot.

Early one morning, at such a gathering spot—a family resort in Hot Springs, Arkansas—I got up, left my teenage children soundly sleeping, and walked barefoot to the pool. My father was already in, the lone lapper. Just walking down the steps and joining my father in his repetitions gave me a feeling of peace

and security. All was well—my father and I were crossing water together.

"Thank you for teaching me to love water," I said
to Dad, as I completed my memorial swim. I was on my
back, weeping and praying. As I moved my arms backwards, I realized my father was still very much with me.
Soon enough, I would be moving forward again.

directions for the cremation and funeral on the Tennessee River

SUSAN LUTHER

Touch the tip of your tongue to my ashes, love;
The acrid dust might yet taste sweet—
Pick up the urn and put it on the pillow
 where I would have slept
For one night more; and kiss me one last kiss.

Then take me to a cooler deep repose
(For ashes not to ashes, dust to dust;
The flowers, songs and mourners
 never were for me—)
Scatter on the water all the burnt remains
Which now are yours as was the flesh
That chose this death.

Then break the vessel.
Bury each small piece so deep
That none will know I'm gone.
I'll take my end now—no more tears,
No sorrow there for me; I want

The green wet silence
Of the Tennessee.

Rottnest Island

SERENA NATHAN

When I was a kid, there were only two ferries that went to Rottnest Island, the Temeraire and the Sea Flyte. They were huge, like the Manly Ferries on the other side of Australia in Sydney. Our family always caught the Temeraire. It went all of eight knots, and although you could see Rottnest Island clearly from the roof of our house near Cottesloe Beach, it took a good hour and a half to get there.

The water surrounding Rottnest is what makes the place so spectacular, and what made it such a special holiday destination for my two little brothers and me. At Narrowneck Bay, the island is so narrow you can sit on your bike in the hot sun and see the Indian Ocean just twenty feet to your left and thirty to your right.

Much as I love to wander around the bays at Rottnest, there is one that deserves the most attention: The Basin. It looks like, well, like a basin. It's a short, five-minute bike ride from the Settlement, and is filled with Perth families like ours every hot Christmas holiday.

I never left home without a snorkel and goggles. In my new bathing suit, a guaranteed annual Christmas present while I was growing up, I would don my equipment, check to make sure I looked like a female Jacques Cousteau (aged ten), and head out along the shallow reef that surrounded The Basin.

This required a walk akin to a daddy longlegs spider, as I tried, in the ankle-deep water, to avoid sharp shells and sucky sea anemones. Once at the ocean end of the reef, I would look up to see my parents lounging on the white sand about a hundred yards away, Mum reading Sylvia Plath's *The Bell Jar* and lighting her cigarette, Dad shading his eyes and gesturing for me to jump in.

I am a Crab, if you follow the stars. That means my birthday is in July and I have a natural affinity for water. You would think that, at this point in the story, I dive in with my snorkel and my goggles and bask in the beauty of my fellow creatures of the deep. Pitifully, I am terrified of doing just that. I'd love to swim with the fish, scamper with the crabs, and loll with the big octopus down there. But what if one of them touched me? It might feel icky. I continue to stand on the edge, watching the party under the sea, wishing I could join in.

Our family continues to spend summer holidays at Rottnest Island. The "family," however, now means my husband, our three small kids, and me. Like my parents, I have a daughter and two younger sons. And, like my parents, I watch my always-cautious daughter, Claudia, stand on the edge of the reef, desperately wanting the courage to jump in. I desperately want her to. I know that there is nothing dangerous in The Basin.

All of a sudden she is in, bobbing up to adjust her goggles and blow extra water out of her snorkel. Look at my ten-year-old female Jacques Cousteau!

I have been perfectly content to lie on the sand (with a good Carol Shields novel and no cigarette) as Claudia skirts the edge of the reef. To face something that terrifies you is the definition of bravery. Now, as I see the brave child looking through her goggles at that city under the reef, I am overcome by the urge to join her.

Grabbing my son Monte's goggles and snorkel, I hobble over the reef of The Basin, still looking like a daddy longlegs, only bigger and faster, and jump in near her. She looks up at me, pulling the snorkel out of her mouth and shouting.

"Mummy, have you seen all the stuff under here? There's a bright orange fish that looks like Nemo!"

I pull Monte's goggles over my eyes and think how they are a bit tight on my forty-year-old head.

"No, darling. Do you know what? I never have. Will you show me?"

And down into the water we dive.

The Waves of Life

BONNIE LOUISE KUCHLER

The waves came in sets, one on top of another, each spinning me in the curl of the surf. Eating sand, gasping for air, I didn't know which way was up. At times, I wanted to give up, but more than that, I wanted to ride the waves. There had to be a way to keep from floundering beneath them!

Looking back at that time in my life, I was floundering in two very different oceans—the big, wet, salty one, and my life.

At home, the waves were my children, their home schooling, my husband, his needs, two dogs, their fleas, and our fledgling business. There was no time to rest between the waves of responsibilities, and I was overwhelmed by the undertow of undone chores. There were times I wanted to run away from that ocean, too.

Finally, in the wet ocean, after dozens of failures, I caught one wave, and then another. Propelled by the smooth rush of water, screaming at the top of my lungs, I realized I'd found a key: *I had to time my launch ahead of the waves!*

When I waited too long to catch a wave, it curled above my head and crashed on top of me, pounding me into the sand. But when I calculated my launch just right, I could kick fiercely for a few seconds, then let the wave carry me the rest of the way.

It wasn't long before I discovered that my life's ocean was not so different—that the same launching-ahead-of-the-waves strategy could work there, too. Organizing took fierce effort, but it was a tiny effort compared to the alternative of drowning in an unrelenting sea of deadlines.

I soon learned that the concept, which was new to me, was as old as the world. It seems that the need for planning and organizing to overcome our tendency to rush into things—in water and life—is common to us all:

Lao Tzu said, *"Prevent trouble before it arises. Put things in order before they exist . . . Rushing into action, you fail."*

The Hindus say, *"Embark upon an action after careful thought. It is folly to say, 'Let us begin the task now and think about it later.'"*

The Shiite Muslims say, *"Success is the result of foresight and resolution; foresight depends upon deep thinking"*

Buddhists say, *"A ship, which is not well prepared, in the ocean goes to destruction, together with its goods and merchants. But when a ship is well prepared, and well joined together, then it does not break up, and all the goods get to the other shore."*

The book of Genesis says, *"Nothing they plan to do will be impossible for them."*

Organizing and planning repaid me with time. Time to relax without a monstrous wall of water chasing my heels, and time to glide with my family and friends. Precious time.

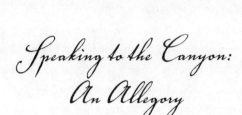

Speaking to the Canyon: An Allegory

Sharon Upp

A dull desert wind brushed carelessly across her flushed cheeks, fingering her hair brusquely as it passed. Rustling through the folds of her copper-colored silk dress, the sound of the wind resembled the tearing of paper.

Her soft slip-on shoes, powdered ochre with sand, blended into the landscape. Saturated with heat, freckled arms shone rose-toned against the barren sky. Sunlight poured over her like thick, drizzled honey and settled in every curve. Suddenly, she melted into a heap at the edge of the canyon, feet dangling into the emptiness below.

With both hands, she lifted her bronze hair upward, feeling a warm gust blow softly across the nape of her neck and upper back. She let her hair go. Sheltering her eyes with a flattened hand, she peeked toward the sun. Quickly dropping her lids and lowering her head, she collapsed inward, completely silent.

Sage, ocotillo, and saguaro breathed in and out, and she imagined she heard an occasional sigh, as if they, too, were tired of the relentless heat, the heaviness of breath, and the weight of their forms. Did they ever worry about rain or crave it in the depths of their souls? Did they ever face the day with dread at the suggestion of withered limbs drying out for lack of moisture? Or

were they infinitely patient and willing to accept whatever came or stayed away?

She wiped her brow free of precious liquid, which
evaporated in rippling waves of heat. Peering down at
her feet, she thought, *How listless they are, suspended there.*
Do they belong to me? She felt the length of her long, thin
arms and examined her outstretched fingers. Her gaze
was detached as she planted her hands on either side of
her, two anchors in the earth. The canyon opened wide
before her, rugged, glowing in raw sienna, burnt umber,
clay and slate, jagged pieces of rock fitting together,
striving upward with great effort. She sighed.

A trickle at the outer edges of her eyes slid down
her cheeks and dropped on her shoulders. In one quick
gesture, she dried her streaked, dusty cheeks. A lifelong habit of hiding, blinking away tears, repeated itself
unconsciously. Soft hands sank back into the dry soil.

Yearning welled up inside her as though a distant
memory of happiness stirred. Where did it come from?
Did it drift from across the canyon? In the shimmering
distance, a place of gardens and rain and music and soft
light whispered to her, *We are here, we are here.*

What she wanted at that moment was for the desert to
sing to her something soothing, comforting. She yearned
for the wind to stroke her hair and soothe her brow. She
ached for a cloud to drift close and embrace her and a
tuft of moss to make soft her ledge. She glanced below.

Speak to me, Canyon, of what you know, her mind sang out.
You sit here patiently as pieces of you fall away in the wind. Do you
miss the particles that crumble or are they dust to you now...shards
long ago forgotten and carried into distances you cannot know?
Will you disappear yourself one day, and does it matter to you? In
the meantime, take a deep breath with me and let it all go.

Empty yourself ricocheted in a thousand harmonic slivers from the jagged edges of the steep ravine. The burning light, shreds of music, copper edges—all exploded in a glorious patchwork symphony before her eyes.

Letting herself release, a deep cavern of frightening images began to well up from inside her, buried from the beginning of time. Courageously, she allowed them to come. Knowing that the canyon had room for them, and knowing that the canyon would not judge her as she had judged herself, she struggled and pushed and breathed into her emptying.

Glancing again into the depths, she released more of her judgments and painful memories. Imagining thousands of pieces of torn paper floating in a spiral to be carried away by the river, she watched her storehouse dissolve. An immense wave of exhaustion engulfed her and she shut her eyes.

Languishing now, she drifted. The scent of orange blossoms and jasmine floated across the air. A dream of gentleness and peace pulled the picture of the sky and canyon, cactus and breezes inward to a speck of light within. A swirling, gentle glow enveloped her mind and heart as she willingly offered her memories, one by one.

Tears escaped, first in a trickle, for they had been tightly guarded. But slowly, allowing them the freedom they so desired, she released a whispering stream. Gathering momentum, the stream yearned to burst into a river.

Suddenly losing all ability to stop the flood, she surrendered. Her grief splashed across her chest, down her legs and eventually formed a perfect waterfall.

No one knows how long she remained there. They know only this: she awoke to a warm, buoyant ocean, which nestled her, surrounded and protected her, nourished, sang to, and loved her. Floating, suspended, she awoke drenched in a precious liquid light that had lain unrecalled, until one day in desperation she spoke to the canyon and it replied, "Empty yourself," and she allowed herself to cry.

Of Trees and Stones Deep Speaking

TONY LUEBBERMANN

With water, a stone may sigh
for the language of stones is naked,
skin-written, rough or smooth,
spoken without the means
a tree has with leaves,
and so articulates instead
by bent water—
the bubbling, the gurgle
for conversation,
the ripple, the eddy for soft laughter,
by waterfall, pride,
and by glittering deep-run pool,
exuberance. Then
there is anger by flood.
      In quiet moments
stones speak by held light;
hold one in your hand,
feel the warm eloquence.

The language of trees
is murmurings,
the rustling rise and fall
of words written in leaf
or gleaming needles
spoken green by the wind
as polysyllabic,
simultaneous passages,

where entire histories
are discussed in a single puff.
(The talk of all our centuries
can pass an afternoon
among the nodding branches of a tree.)
          And when stilled
In the gold autumn light,
their voice is more than radiant:
touch a leaf, see brilliance pain—
countless tinctures
in each leaf's verse.

With language, comes silence:
the air wheels smoke,
birds fall, fish bob belly-white
against the smutty stone.
          Winter parses;
words, snow-weighted, slow.

We hold bizarre pieties,
our language for these states,
our disjoint grammars
for water, air, fire, ice.
We have no cognates,
no verbs to join,
so the babbling separation is ours,
but ours alone,
for deep kernels, ripe kernels thresh
in the shouting, word-filled rain,
when each tree, each stone,
with each bright tear,
          speak and rejoin.

Feel the Power

KELLY KARGES

The ocean moves me. Folly Beach, riding the waves on boogie boards. First, Dad, my brothers, and me, floating with our boards and watching the horizon for the right wave. Then, seeing it coming and paddling like crazy to catch it at just the right spot.

There is nothing like the power of a great wave that literally slams you toward the shore, carries you so hard that all you can do is hang on for the ride. You grip your fingers into that board and hope it lasts, hope it doesn't turn you over and pound you into the sand.

Then my children want to "ride the waves too, Daddy." I set them on the board and stand waist-deep in the surf and hold them there until the right wave comes along.

I try to let them go at just the right moment and hear them scream in delight as the wave carries their light little bodies all the way to shore and gently deposits them on the beach. They jump up and run back yelling, "Again, Daddy, again!"

Maybe I've forgotten how I'm just riding the waves of God's grace in my life. Out here on the plains of Nebraska it's easy to forget what the pounding of the surf sounds like—easy to forget the awesome undertow that lifts you off your feet and drags you along.

Maybe I've forgotten how you can float for a long time, thirty feet from shore, waiting for the tide to turn and the big waves to crank up again. Maybe my landlocked mind needs to remember how forces beyond me can provide the wave that I jump onto and it'll carry me all the way in.

Maybe I've forgotten that there is a danger to choosing to ride that board; that you can break your neck if the wrong set of circumstances converges on you and your board at just the wrong time.

But it's the thrill of the ride that sends you running back out there, against the surf, backing through the waves that'll knock you down if you don't take them straight on.

Scanning the horizon, you look for signs in the undulating water that tell you a crest is going to break and start rolling toward you; that just the right circumstances are going to come together at just the right time, and you are there to hitch a ride and fly through the water, a human slingshot at the beach.

Tasting the salt, you rub your chest raw from the board, but you can't stop. It's hard to describe. It has the elements of preaching a great sermon, riding the bull for eight seconds, jumping out of the swing at its peak.

I forget sometimes that it's God's grace that carries me through forgiveness to healing. I forget that aqua flying feeling; that it's not me. I don't have to do anything, just be there and jump on when the right wave presents itself. And if I miss that perfect wave, wait a minute; another one will come along. I can just be. That is enough.

The power of God is beyond me. It's so great it scares me. But I can't help but run right back out into it, straight at it, in hopes of catching another ride. There is nothing like it. Ride the wave. Feel the power, God's power, to take me and move me and throw me toward the shore.

Tide Pools

CHERISE WYNEKEN

"Don't forget to see the tide pools," our son called, as we waved goodbye.

My thoughts went to our honeymoon and other happy times searching for treasures among the tide pools along the California coast. They had always been a special part of our trips to that area—promising to show us secrets from deep within the sea. The tide never failed.

We were on our way to Acadia National Park in Maine. According to our son, the tide pools were fantastic there, and I aimed to see them. I could almost hear the roar of rollers chasing each other—the hiss as they broke on rock—feel the spray on my cheek, see green-tressed seaweed maids curtsy to the cresting waves.

"You aren't going to pull one of your 'it's too late' control tactics when we get to the park and tide pools—are you?" I asked Alex, my husband.

"You make me sound like a villain."

Alex and I had been married forever. I'd become a pro at balancing. When to talk, when to turn it off, when to push for something, when to let it lie. We drove along in our brown Mercedes, silent. Alex, at the wheel since 4:00 A.M., stared at the road ahead, probably hearing Bach's Fugue in D, not breakers.

Buttercups spilled yellow across green fields. Pink and purple larkspur filled roadside gutters with their steepled spires. Ads displayed phrases I'd never seen before: barn sales, kayaks for sale, whale watching tours by air. We crossed onto L'Isle des Monts Desert. Alex reached into the side pocket and handed me a travel book. "I've marked a few motels I think are good. Watch for one of them."

I gave him a salute.

He darted me a quick look. "You want to choose? Go ahead. See how easy it is without studying first."

Give him a break, I thought. *He's tired.* "Here's a nice one in Bar Harbor," I replied.

"Too far from the ferry," he said. "We want to catch the first one out to Nova Scotia in the morning. Here's one that I checked—hillside inn with view." We pulled in and registered.

"Let's drive into Bar Harbor and check out a place to eat tonight. Going to treat you to some real Maine lobster," Alex said.

"I thought we were going to the park."

"I need some gas."

I looked at my watch. "Will there be time to stop at the tide pools?"

"Yeah. Sure."

We freshened up. Drove into Bar Harbor. Hunted out a place to eat lobster. Watched the boats perch on the bay like a flock of ibis in the Everglades. Pulled into a gas station. Alex and the old timer filling the tank began to talk.

You'd think they were long lost friends. He's stalling—tide pools were never *in his plans.*

"Let's check out the Information Center first," he said, as we finally entered Acadia Park.

"Now? How come you're suddenly interested in Information Centers?"

Hands full of pamphlets and maps, we began circling the one-way road. Slim white-skinned birch trees peeped wide-eyed from deep within sun-specked woods. Cottonwoods turned silver dollar leaves, catching the echo of a jingling breeze. Wild roses flirted along the path. Frenchman Bay lay quiet—drenched in blue.

It's not like I imagined—but it has a certain balance.

"Here," I said, pointing to a long stretch of beach. "This looks like a good place to stop."

Alex kept driving.

"How about here?"

"Uh-uh."

"You're going too fast. We pass the pools before we see them."

"Uh-huh."

I reached for the park map. "A good spot's coming up. Slow down."

"Everyone else thinks so, too. Look at the crowd. There isn't room to park."

We drove on in static silence until we came to a section of the shore lined with huge smooth boulders.

"STOP. I'm going to look—even if you're not."

Alex pulled to the side of the road. "I'll wait."

"Whatever."

I turned onto a roadside path toward an opening in the brush and struck out across the boulders for the shore. At last I was down—standing at the edge. No shallow pools spawning sea anemones and starfish. No crashing waves—just the ones inside. *What makes him think he can always have his way?*

I sat down and watched the water lap beneath my feet. The quiet backwash roll calmed my angry feelings. Andante and allegro—a steady ebb and flow. It reminded me of my dad's oft-repeated advice: "Marriage isn't a fifty-fifty proposition. It's more like seventy-five–seventy-five." *Good and bad overlapping—like the waves.* Some garbage had drifted into my day, but sea anemones and starfish would be there, too.

Once again, the ocean had brought me a treasure: a wider view that helped me cope with my problems at hand. The tide never fails.

Under the Surface

HELEN M. SADLER

On a new moon Saturday in late November, the skies over northeastern Ohio were gray and the air had a chill. I walked the trail through the woods near my home, a winding path through deciduous trees and pine forest.

I strolled along, kicking the leaves, taking in familiar sights and sounds. The trees were bare and the leaves were ankle-deep on the ground, pungent with the woodsy smell of rot as they returned to the earth. In the distance, I heard the honking of wild geese as they migrated to a brighter place for the winter. I had only more gray days to look forward to, more cold, and probably plenty of snow.

At the end of the woods sat a lake surrounded by trees and picnic tables. My usual course was to walk right past the lake and straight to my car, drive home, and record in my journal what transpired on my walk: usually a message from within, a creative thought, or a course of action I might want to take. On this Saturday, despite the cold, I found myself sauntering over to a table alongside the lake.

At age forty-two, I was beginning to feel the effects of midlife. The previous few years had been chaotic and demanding, and I now felt myself at a place where I could choose a new direction.

This was a solitary act if I ever knew one. I was certain

I could figure it out, even though I had only a vague idea of what it might look like. I was convinced that whatever it was would come to me in a blinding flash, so I just had to wait for that moment. The wide expanse of lake reflecting the somber skies seemed to match the murkiness I felt about my direction.

As I sat there, I watched six wild geese floating about randomly. They gathered together in a group and began to create a united voice, swimming from one lake edge to the other.

Listening to their calls, I was reminded of what poet Mary Oliver says about the sound of the wild geese—"harsh and exciting," announcing their place in the family of things.

I felt a kind of communion with the geese as they toured the lake. Once they reached the opposite edge, they turned around, again in unison, and it appeared they were going to swim back to where they came, like lap swimmers in a pool.

To my surprise, they suddenly took flight, in complete unison, the singing and calling continuing for several minutes afterward, as they flew toward new destinations, to warmer climates that would nourish them in the months to come.

I spent nearly an hour by Longwood Lake that day, coming to no conclusions about anything. Once home, I dutifully recorded my encounter with the geese, then promptly forgot about it as I got on with my day. I was a member of a local club and had some phone calls to make to members. One person I called, a friend named David, was home, and we got into a conversation on career matters.

"Helen, you should go back to school and become a teacher. You'd be so good," he said.

I quickly denounced the idea as unworkable. After all, I had no college credits to my name, and with my current financial situation, the thought of attending college was completely outside the bounds of my imagination.

Yet, David's suggestion didn't leave me. For a month, I struggled with it, fought with myself over it, and loudly cursed him in the dark for mentioning it. Something under the surface was rising, something I could no longer deny.

One afternoon, desperate and alone, I found myself in my car, the heater running full blast, windshield wipers beating back wet snow, looking out across a frozen Longwood Lake. Snow lay on its surface and on the picnic table where I sat watching the geese just a few short weeks before.

I honestly don't know what drew me to the lake—I don't even remember deciding to go there. I shut off the car and made my way through the falling snow to a wooden fishing pier. I climbed the stairs slowly, methodically, marking my way in the snow.

I looked out across the white lake and thought about this thing bouncing around inside me, the long-held dream I never dared to dream: my desire to be a teacher. It was as if a thick layer of ice held it under the surface for more years than I cared to recount.

With one swift stroke, David had broken through that ice. I had spent a lot of energy trying to fix the hole he made, instead of looking at what was seeping up to the surface. In a moment of surrender, with swirling snowflakes surrounding me, I softly said, "Yes."

I live in southwest Florida now. No wild geese visit me here. Instead, I am graced with great blue herons, snowy egrets, bald eagles, and common moorhens, all of whom come to the water for nourishment. Nearly seven years have passed since those days by Longwood Lake. Like the geese, I have found a warmer climate, a place that deeply nourishes my spirit. I have also found much more.

As I reflect on that November day in Ohio, I am convinced that mysterious forces were at work, causing a major change in my life. My time by the water created an opening, and along with the right words from a friend and a great deal of inner struggle, I found something that wasn't lost, but was hiding.

I discovered this simple truth: finding one's passion is a sacred act because it happens communally. No blinding revelations are required—just an open mind and a willingness to listen to that thing that calls to you from the depths.

This year I graduate from college with a bachelor's degree, and will begin teaching middle school. The lake on which I now live continues to teach me about the family of things, the life we don't expect, the places at which we never thought we'd actually arrive.

Like the wild geese, we may seem to be floating randomly on the water of our lives. But our Calling calls to us, causing us to lift our wings and fly, singing in unison with others, beating our way toward our previously unimagined dreams, and the pursuit of our fantastic passions.

Meditation:

SACRED WATER AND SACRED IMAGINATION

Do you feel stuck? Have you temporarily lost that feeling of being in the flow of life, aligned with the great rhythms of the universe? Are you struggling to make a decision about "what's next" in your life?

For the next seven days, include images of water in your meditations. You might want to use the first day's meditation to let your own images of water come to you. At the end of your meditation time, have pen and paper handy to jot down what you saw, felt, and experienced.

You can also use some of these images, in any order you wish:

~ A serene lake

~ A wishing well

~ An ancient grotto

~ A sparkling ocean

~ A tropical waterfall

~ A flowing river

~ A deep, still pool

~ A thunderstorm

~ A gentle rain

~ A rushing creek

When you meditate with these images, don't just picture them in your mind. Use all of your senses to put yourself into the water-filled scene. Hear the sound of the roaring waterfall or gently lapping waves; feel the salt spray or the cool raindrops. Dive under and become one with the water, or simply walk beside it. Let your inner water journey take you to new and unexpected places where you can once again feel the flow of your own soul's rhythms.

Part Two

WATER MEMORIES:
STORIES OF RECOLLECTION
AND REMINISCENCE

Ocean Child

MARIL CRABTREE

I grew up far from the coasts. My first view, at age nine, of a vast expanse of water—the Gulf of Mexico—created a permanent shift in me, a deep connection with the mysteries of endless waves lapping at my feet.

On that family vacation, I took to this new thrill called "ocean" with all the enthusiasm of a child discovering a new friend. I knew how to swim, so I swam out as far as I dared and floated back in. I loved the buoyancy of floating in salt water. I'd always had a little difficulty getting my body to float in a pool, but this was different. I felt carried along in gentle bliss—until the moment when a larger-than-usual wave slapped over me and interrupted my fantasies.

Abruptly I came up vertical—in time to be slapped by another wave, this one forcing me underwater. I surfaced again, sputtering and trying to gain some balance in this new game my friend wanted to play.

The waves propelled my body toward shore, their gentle rocking motion transformed into relentless pounding. I felt the sand beneath me and thought I had been spared more abuse, but at my back another wave slapped me down into the churning, sandy depths. Each time I lifted my head out for a quick gulp of air, the waves pushed me down again. I swallowed so much salt water I thought I might drown—even in three feet of water.

Finally, I struggled all the way into shore, beyond reach of those powerful, playful, yet punishing waves. I lay in the sand, gasping for breath, and was happy to spend the rest of the day building sandcastles and wading in knee-deep water.

I didn't want to give up the friendship, though, and I devoted the rest of my vacation to finding out what I needed to know to cooperate with the waves and currents, instead of ignoring or resisting them. I learned how to feel the water's rhythms, how to pay attention to timing, and how to align my body with the tempo and direction of the waves.

I never forgot that experience. Eventually, it became a metaphor for my spiritual life. Just as the laws of nature apply to physical matter, spiritual "laws" and principles apply to metaphysical matter. I discovered that the universe, like the ocean, can be a playful or a punishing experience, depending on how I align myself with its powerful, impersonal laws. I found that, if I respect the universe enough to learn how to live in accord with those laws, they will carry me far; if I ignore those spiritual laws, they have the potential to make life an endless, perhaps even deadly, struggle.

I'm grateful for that first experience with sacred mother ocean. While less than blissful, it gave me an invaluable lesson that has often guided me to pause, listen, and seek understanding, rather than plunge in without preparation. I learned the wisdom of aligning myself with the power of the universe, in the same way that I learned to flow with the tide, not against it.

Now, when things aren't going well, I ask myself if I've done the spiritual work of aligning my intentions with those cosmic laws that move as predictably as ocean tides.

Trial by Water

SHERRY NORMAN HORBATENKO

Summers were long and hot where we grew up, in the hills of central Florida. Clermont was a small town nestled into an area known as Land O' Lakes. My brothers, sister, and I, along with hundreds of other kids, spent every possible moment of every possible day in the water somewhere in those lakes.

A lot of people knew their kids were at the lakeside beaches swimming, boating, and fishing, but only a few knew that there was a rite of passage among us kids. One step of this initiation rite was to swim the canals connecting the lakes. This was not the wisest thing to do. We were in Florida, after all: land of alligators and snakes.

Lake Minneola is one of the larger lakes in a chain of eleven canal-connected lakes ranging in size from twenty to 3,634 acres. To swim Lake Minneola, a lake of 1,888 acres, was the final step. You could start from the shore or jump from the dock, whichever made you the most comfortable.

The goal was directly across: a set of railroad trestles spanning the connecting canal to Lake Minnehaha. You had to be extra careful when you reached the other side because of the rocks—lots of them—that you had to negotiate before you could pull yourself ashore under the trestles. Luckily, there was usually someone around in a boat who would pick you up to bring you back in your moment of glory.

The summer my brother, Larry, decided to make this swim he was really too young. This was generally considered to be within the realm of the older teens. Six weeks before his attempt he had been severely beaten by one of the older boys for daring to talk to the boy's girlfriend. After the police had been called and arrived to break up the fight, I remember standing in knee-deep water, holding my brother's head while blood poured from his nose, and telling the winner what a *big, brave man* he was to have managed to beat up someone four years younger, a head and a half shorter, and about eighty pounds lighter. Half the kids at the beach that day followed us to the hospital. Most of the same kids were there when Larry and his friend John decided—without telling anyone—to make their bid for the other side of the lake.

I was playing in the shallow water with my three younger siblings, two small boys and a girl, when I looked around and realized that Larry wasn't with us. Concerned, I began calling for him. The calls quickly became screams, and the snack bar attendant realized I was serious. He ran to the end of the pier and searched the water. We were still searching when the police arrived a few minutes later.

They put a boat into the water, and it began circling the area in long, slow sweeps. A boy said that he'd heard two guys talking about swimming to the other side of the lake, but no one knew for certain if they'd done so.

After a short conference, the boat headed for the railroad trestles on the other side of the lake. When the boat was only a small speck on the water, it made a circle and started back slowly. It seemed to take forever to make its way back. Standing there on the end of the pier, watching that speck, I nearly fell in when someone said next to me, "Did they find him?"

I turned to find John beside me. I asked, "What do you mean? What are you doing here?"

He said, "We made it all the way there, and Larry wanted to swim back."

I demanded, "And why aren't you *with* him?"

I didn't mean to sound accusing. I didn't even mean to scream at him, but at that point there wasn't anything I could handle being but angry, and John *was* the older of the two. He was a preacher's son, for crying out loud. He should have known better. He should have told me what Larry was planning to do.

He said, "I'm sorry. I didn't think I could make it all the way back, and Larry wouldn't listen to me. I came to get a boat to go back and get him, but it looks like someone's already out there with him."

It took more than an hour for Larry to swim the last half of the distance with that boat and those two police officers watching over him, but he made it. All the way to the shore. He was so tired he crawled out.

That night, when asked if he'd learned anything from such a stunt, he said, "Yes. Perseverance. Don't look back. Just focus straight ahead and keep on reaching and pulling, reaching and pulling. You pull until you've pulled all the water behind you."

Dad asked him how he got that bit of wisdom, and Larry said, "That's what that police officer kept saying over and over to me; let the water carry you home. Just reach and pull, reach and pull."

It was the same officer who had answered the call when the bullyboy beat up Larry six weeks earlier. I believe the police officer understood my brother's need that day, and that's why they didn't just drag him into the boat and haul him to shore.

Larry was never beaten again. He walked taller. Our parents let him go without punishment. Two years later, he set a new record in track for the two-mile race.

In the Woods, 1951

CHARLES ADÉS FISHMAN

I remember how the light pawed down
through densely tangled branches
and how the narrow creek jangled
over its scatter of burnished stones
worn to a smoothness in the cold churn
of water. The day began when school ended

and our feet sank into fern banks
and leaf-mulch or squelched in bog-holes
of aromatic muck. We leapt over moss-
crushed oaks white-barked paper birches
climbed wind-sheared hickories and beeches

and, in the green drench of summer,
swam naked in our garden. In that clear water
that granted every pardon, we gashed our hearts
and came up gasping, the afternoon sun

encircling our foreheads with tendrils of molten gold.
We heard drums in the leaf-tops that spoke of endings,
yet we lived as if time was not our master, as if

we were kings of the forest and not its slowly drowning sons.

Water Tap

Margaret E. Lynch

After entering the grounds, I drive my car into the near-est parking lot.

No spaces are delineated on the cracked and crum-bling pavement where shoots of wild grass sprout in the narrow spaces. My mind takes a poetic turn, quoting snippets of Tennyson's "Flower in the Crannied Wall." No wonder, I think. My purpose in coming here *is* rather poetic.

The cemetery lies uphill, a short distance away. *In Flanders Fields the poppies grow / Between the crosses row on row,* I recall. There are openings in the surrounding hedges; I enter through one of them recollected from the past. It is near the water tap where I used to sit, sip, and talk with friends—a place where we would surreptitiously meet on days of silent retreat to share and reveal.

I fill the paper cup I have brought with me, sit down, and sample the water. But I am disappointed. It's not as cold or refreshing as I remember it.

My thoughts return to those times past when, among other young women of like mind and heart, I began a journey aimed at the merger of my "I" into the communal "we" through a Catholic religious congregation of nuns, the Sisters of Charity.

We spent the first three years on the grounds of the sisters' Motherhouse—also the campus of the College of

St. Elizabeth—where we prayed, studied, and learned the behaviors expected of us. Initial monthly days of recollection expanded, after the three-year preparatory period, into an annual requisite week of silent retreat—a challenge to us vibrant, active young women. Those who wanted to talk, we agreed, would meet at the water tap in the cemetery. Here we would be undisturbed by those in authority.

Often over the next few years, we needed the feedback and solace of friends during these times of "silent" retreat. It was the 1960s; self-growth and social awareness, reality and disillusionment with religious institutions gradually replaced the old certainties. Our number of water-gatherers grew smaller as many of us readied to leave the community and continue our lives beyond its restrictions.

Today, the spot is silent and I am alone. I begin my pilgrimage among the uniform white crosses; their number startles me. I notice that the grass is well trimmed, but only a few of the graves have flowers on them or show any signs of personal attention. In my mind, I hear voices from the '60s questioning and lamenting, "Where have all the flowers gone . . . "

I look for names and dates on the crosses, searching for those to whom I never said thank you or goodbye, for women who deserve to hear me say "I'm sorry" or "I forgive you."

I find the markers for the woman who taught me secretarial skills, and the English teacher I so admired and tried to imitate. I tell each of them how useful and valuable their contributions were. Then, I locate the graves of two young women I knew who died in their twenties from undiagnosed and untreated illnesses. Anger stirs in me; I quell it by asking each of them if they felt it was worthwhile. I tell them I hope they have come into their glory, mention my aging sense of muddling through, and ask them to drop my name to the Big Guy.

The search for specific gravesites becomes burdensome, so I abandon it. Instead, I meander about the cemetery and inadvertently come upon other, long-forgotten names. When I stumble across the gravesite of a former superior, memorable for her meanness and lack of compassion, an old familiar fear tightens my stomach. I tell her she is forgiven, but, questioning my own sincerity, I move quickly on.

My spirit lightens when I find the grave of my kindergarten teacher who personified the beauty and kindness of the Virgin Mary, and I respond to her with, "And a very happy good morning to you!"

A whispered "I'm sorry" greets a competent principal whose practicality and common sense I had undervalued in my search for perfection and intellectual prowess.

I reach the place of entry and turn toward the rows of crosses. No one is watching, I hope, as I extend my arms across the field. "Rest in peace," I say, making the sign of the cross over all of them, these sisters whose vowed religious commitment I had at one time shared.

At the water tap, I stop for a final drink. Somehow, it tastes better. I feel cleansed by the peace of acceptance and reconciliation. Graced and empowered, I squeeze out through the hedges and walk away.

Breaking the Drought

VIVIENNE MACKIE

We lived in South Africa in the 1980s in the middle of a terrible prolonged drought. In the summers, the supposed rainy season, we'd watch the sky hopefully every afternoon, wondering if that cloud, that wisp, would build up and become a rain cloud. Mostly it didn't, and everything got drier and drier.

Bush fires sprang up daily. Smoke and bits of blackened plants clogged clothes, noses, and mouths, stinging eyes and giving many people a continual hacking cough. Dams dried up, gardens died, parched earth cracked, hundreds of farm animals died, and water rationing became a fact of life.

At first, rationing meant that no swimming pools were filled, no one could wash cars using a garden hose, and we couldn't water our gardens. Then it got more serious. We learned to count out our daily ration, just enough to cook with and drink, with a little left over for washing.

People shared many tricks to help eke out the little water available. When a tap was turned on, no drop of water ever went down the drain: we collected every droplet and used it for brushing our teeth, or adding to bath water, or washing clothes or dishes.

The water from our two-inch-deep bath stayed in the bathtub, and we bailed it out with a bucket and put it into the toilet cistern. Toilet bowls sprouted amazingly colorful growths, but at least we could flush a couple of times a day.

On wonderful luxury days, we had a very quick shower, but the water drained through a special hose directly onto the garden. I'm not sure how much the plants and the lawn liked soapy water, but that's what they got.

People got tired of never being really clean, of counting every drop, and tempers became frayed. We all got hotter and our lives drier and drier. We started to snap at each other, to watch our neighbors to make sure they weren't using more than their ration. We almost forgot what it was like to have water readily available, but a deep memory persisted and we carried on hoping and watching the skies.

One afternoon, the weather did build up; the slight wisp in the sky became a white ball, a darker ball, a bigger bank of actual clouds, a dense black sheet. We saw lightning, heard thunder. Will it come here, to our neighborhood, to our garden, we wondered? It did.

The happiness was indescribable. Not only did the skies open up to bring rain, that wonderful wet stuff, it also relieved our tension. We ran outside and welcomed the rain, faces up to receive the drops. The kids stripped to underwear and cavorted happily. Even adults were happy to be drenched. We whooped and shouted, did a kind of rain dance on our front lawn. The cool drops tingled our skin and cleansed our bodies. It was the kind of rain that gushes over the top of rain gutters, in such a hurry to hit the earth it has no time to go down the spout.

I am always mesmerized by rainfall. I get lost in the sound and sight of the heavens washing away the dirt and dust of the world, and even more so that special day. As I watched my kids, memories of running in the rain, of carefree splashing, also came pouring in, a welcome reprieve from the extreme worries of the drought and what it was doing to our country.

Blessed relief: the parched earth soaked up the water and we smelled that wonderful scent of hot, dry earth cooled by rain—pungent, spicy. Some garden plants almost instantaneously stopped drooping, and I swear my lawn looked greener.

After the storm passed, the sun came out, the air sparkled, and the flying ants appeared—suddenly. Where had they been hiding all this time? Hundreds of them, more likely thousands, fluttered and clustered around bushes and moved on. Our kids chased them gleefully, reminding their dad about his memories of catching them as a child and roasting them over an outside fire in Rhodesia.

In celebration, we decided to do the same. The flying ants got crispy on the fire, and a wonderful aroma filled our garden. The kids, my husband, and I pulled the wings off each flying ant and popped the whole thing in our mouths. They were crunchy, chewy, delicious, sort of salty-buttery, with bodies the size of a piece of popcorn.

They were a feast from the rain, because the rain released them. That storm brought more than just water—it brought coolness, emotional relief, and a tasty African snack!

It was raining

W. K. BUCKLEY

when your water broke—the color pearl,
a five-day spell in the heat of June
as the lake roared around the mill/ . . . & then,
a little gnome—dangling in the hands,
his head revolving like a moon, legs strong enough for
horse/ . . . you hold him in a shadow
like an elm/& you take him bundles to the waves
that remind you of his growth, of the purl in muscle/

Now, to see him by the waves, his chest to breakers—
the waters whirling in his ear when comes the rite of birth:
his breaking from you
his private rain & we are

Dew-Kissed

KATHALEEN MCKAY

The gully path winds down from my street into the park. When day breaks, the summer sun rises over the thick, tree-lined banks, creating channels of warm light. Shadows, designed by the rusty train trestle that looms to the north, dance across the grassy edges of the soccer field. The magic of the geometric shapes projected across the wet grass welcomes the imagination. To walk through them is like walking in a dream.

From time to time, one's path links to another person—a fellow human who yearns for the quiet space between daybreak and breakfast. Someone out enjoying a brisk walk around the park, barefoot in dew-kissed grass.

A shoeless, middle-aged woman I encounter one particular morning is radiant. "This feels SO good on the feet!" She urges me to try it out.

My own toes, by this time, are swimming in soggy socks. The temptation to untie my sneakers and peel them off is hard to resist, but my time is short today, so I decide to wait until my next visit.

Not long after that, the image of the barefoot woman at the park wanders through my mind. Years of standing at work have left my feet vulnerable to discomfort, and as the hours pass, during my shift at the store, they begin to ache. My right heel throbs by the end of the evening. It feels like a fiery stone is embedded under the skin. I can imagine the relief of feeling the cool, dew-drenched blades of grass.

I rise early the following morning, energized by a sense of anticipation. Heading toward the park, I spot the glistening strands of a spider's web among the delicate stems of Queen Anne's lace. Beads of dew cling to its fine-woven threads. I am reminded of the magnificence of creation in each perfect droplet in the spider's masterpiece. Such gems offer the human eye a spectacular glimpse of water in its natural splendor. Every solitary glint gleams like a single diamond of the sea.

The park is empty as I gaze across the inviting blanket of green. I feel a delicious sense of freedom as I toss my shoes and socks into a bag and begin my barefoot odyssey. My toes sink into the soft blades and the dew tickles my weary soles as I connect with both water and earth. *When did I last feel like this?* I wonder. In the peace of the morning, I return to the summers of childhood and see myself running through arcs of water, spouting from our backyard sprinkler . . . giggling.

A surge of playful energy enlivens every pore as the loose grass clings to my skin, transforming my feet into a pair of shaggy green slippers. They are a perfect fit for my barefoot odyssey!

The Waters of Childhood

PATTI TANA

When I think of the waters of childhood, the river comes first to my mind. The streets of Peekskill rose on the east bank of the Hudson River like trees with roots in the water. My house was only two blocks from the river—two steep, long, winding blocks up a street everyone called Snake Hill. In a town built on hills, this one was famous. Too treacherous for cars in the ice-covered snow, Snake Hill was claimed by children sledding all the way down to the railroad station by the river.

The regular click of the wheels on the tracks and deep-throated cries of train whistles carried me south along the river to New York City and north toward Poughkeepsie and the country beyond. I'd sit by the window and watch the flow of the river as the train swept me along. The water was smooth gray-green if I looked directly sideward out my window, yet shimmering blue if I looked out the window of the seat in front of me. We'd pass tugboats pushing their huge flat loads, and sometimes on the western shore a silver engine pulled long white cars like the tail of a nearby comet.

Riding home from Grand Central Station, after the dark tunnel and the massive blocks of shadowy buildings, a narrow lane of water reflected whatever light was left in the sky. At first pinched by sheer palisades, the river quickly widened beneath ridges of gray boulders bulging through masses of trees, and then opened to the smooth layers of the Ramapo Mountains in shades of purple at nightfall.

The train moved swiftly past Dobbs Ferry and Tarrytown, past Sing Sing where my father served time before he met my mother. Always it paused at Harmon to change engines. Always the hiss of the steam and the small, sudden jolt as the cars coupled. And then the slow, gentle rocking motion of those last few miles home.

When the trees were bare I could see the river from Mother's bedroom window. To the south lay the Ghost Fleet, large gray warships, where tons of rotting wheat were stored. Northward on the opposite shore was Bear Mountain State Park. On clear winter nights, I could see lights outlining the ski jump and flames from a skier's moving torch splitting the dark space between the lights.

Until my parents divorced when I was ten, we often went with my father to Bear Mountain Park for his summer weekend job as security guard. The State of New York saw fit to issue my father a gun, so I grew up with a gun in the top drawer of his dresser, where he could grab it as easily as a pair of socks. To reach Bear Mountain Bridge, he drove north over precarious mountain roads, often skirting ledges and stone walls. He made every trip a race—tires screeching, horn blasting—and we were his captives. Mother sat bolted next to him begging him to slow down. In the back my big brother sat up straight, knuckles white on the back of the sat in front of him, while I crouched down with my arms around my little brother. I'd peek out to see how far we had to go, and when I saw the river again I knew we were almost safe.

While Father roamed the park grounds in mirrored sunglasses and olive uniform, gun on hip, Mother took us to the playground, the zoo, the pool, and my favorite place—the lake. Hessian Lake was surrounded by tall pines and weeping willows whose slender branches bent down to the water. Near the rowboats, a plaque explained that the lake was named after the German mercenary soldiers who were hired by the British during the Revolutionary War. The colonists sank their boats as they rowed across the lake and their bodies were never found, giving rise to the legend that Hessian Lake is bottomless. It pleased me to think that here was a place where hired assassins could be made to vanish.

I'd walk around the lake and find a quiet place to sit and look at the reflections in the water. Around the rim, the trees doubled in length in fluid shadows. The large, moving surface gently distorted the tone of the sky and patches of clouds. Every breeze gave texture to the water, and sun highlighted the shifting patterns.

If I drew close, I would see a pale oval face, freckled as a fish. Small earrings where a gypsy had pierced, dark braided hair, teeth in braces that never did close the gap between them. Eyes the same changeable green as the lake, and, like the lake, flecked with gold.

Beneath the surface of the water, another world: fleeting tadpoles and fuzzy moss on stones that looked in shifting, filtered light like tiny forests on small islands. I'd find a stone and toss it high, then watch it fall in the water, imagining it falling forever.

Consumed and Cleansed

KATHY COUDLE KING

It was one of the perfect spring days we dream of in North Dakota in the dead of winter. Spacious blue skies encircling our heads, a whisper of warm wind against our arms, and the chorus of birds freshly returned from their winter homes.

Except it wasn't a perfect day. My husband and I were pushing the double-stroller with our two toddlers around the block. We were looking for signs that the neighbors were still present. What we found were dark houses, empty driveways, silent streets. Everyone had evacuated but us, our stoic Norwegian neighbor, and his Cree wife. They, like us, didn't think it would get that bad. We were several miles from the river. We weren't in danger of the floodwaters that had already broken through the dike the night before. Alan and I were making plans to run to the market to stock up on food—just in case—when a stranger drove by in a minivan.

"Hurry up! The water's coming! You've got to evacuate!"

The man barely slowed down as he yelled out to us, panic thick in his voice. Without discussing it, we raced home, throwing clothing into suitcases and hauling a few odds and ends up from the finished basement where I had my office. I grabbed a few computer disks, no plan in mind, no priorities of what to take and what to leave.

I shoved into my pocket a few toy knights for my three-year-old son, grabbed my one-year-old daughter's favorite doll. Where would we go? How long would we be gone? The university where we worked had canceled classes to help build sandbag dikes. If we were evacuating, clearly classes would be canceled, as we were mere blocks from the campus.

We could go anywhere, take the vacation in Montana we'd talked about. We could visit my family in Ohio, his family in Louisiana. We got in our car and began to drive west, with no real plan in mind except to get away from the river water that was threatening to consume our town.

About an hour later, we heard the unimaginable on the car radio. Downtown was on fire. Fire trucks were immersed in water, but they couldn't get the fire under control. It leapt from one historic building to the next. Helicopters flew over, dumping water from above, while yards away the river spilled over the dikes, creating waterfalls on the prairie landscape. It was unbelievable. Would the whole town be lost in this wrath of water and fire?

Another hour later, we stopped for the night and turned on CNN. There was our town of 50,000 on television. Many Americans can't find North Dakota on a map, and there was our little town plastered all over the national news. It was said to be the largest evacuation per capita since Atlanta during the Civil War. As we watched workers motor in boats through city streets to rescue people from their flooded homes, we knew we would not see Montana that year.

The next day we turned our vehicle around and headed east. We would wait out the evacuation in Minnesota. Detours due to the flooding fields turned a four-hour trip into eight. Finally, we reached a resort where the owners gave us the largest cabin they had for the price of the smallest. News of the flood had preceded us, and communities as far away as the Twin Cities opened their arms to flood evacuees.

A week went by and we weren't sure how we would continue to afford the cabin rental, when neighbors from home tracked us down. They knew a woman who had a lake home to spare. We could stay there as long as we needed it. The name of the lake? Grace. While the angry Red River, swollen with the snow of eight blizzards, seemed to be trying to consume our hometown, this still half-frozen lake offered us shelter, offered us grace. There was room enough for two busy children, our cat, and our two basset hounds. There was space enough for us to breathe and regroup.

When we were finally able to return home three weeks later, the ice had melted on the lake and the fishing season was commencing. A few days before we returned to Grand Forks to pump out the eight feet of water that filled our basement, the dogs began to trumpet in that way unique to hounds.

I glanced out the window to see them straining at their leashes. What was all the ruckus? Outside, I found another four-legged critter. A turtle plodded up the ramp leading to our front door! Her shell was the size of a dinner plate, mossy green, and she moved her gray-brown head from side to side, like a driver trying to find a particular house on an unfamiliar street. She had clearly taken a wrong turn, and where had she ended?

Ever the city girl, I squealed with delight. Then, sure of what I needed to do, I ran back into the house. Grabbing a pair of rubber gloves, I ran back outside and picked up the turtle gingerly. With the children in tow, the dogs cheering behind me, I walked to the lake's edge and set the turtle in the water.

Whether or not this was where she wanted to go, she didn't hesitate but slid away from us in a moment. She'd find her way home. We would, too, although home had changed quite a bit.

Home had a watermark on its side, just as there's a watermark on the souls of all who survived the flood of '97. Today, we have a greater sense of community, know the gratitude of a hot meal delivered by the American Red Cross, know the kindness of strangers who sent toys and clothes. We know the monetary gifts of people like McDonald's heiress Joan Kroc. They showed up on doorsteps with water pumps in hand, ready to empty our soggy homes. We know there are angels who walk the earth: none wore wings, but some wore waders.

And all the material possessions we piled as high as ten feet tall on the curbs of our streets—all that stuff we lost—we know it was just that: stuff. We let it go, learned we could let it go, learned that what we had gained from the flood waters that spring was ever so much more precious. First, the river consumed us, but in the end, it cleansed us.

Grace

ANNE CORAY

There—just where the rivulet
meets expanse of lake,
let us gather like gulls turned inland,
all of us—our infant and middle-aged
selves, and those parts that are older,
sadder or not. Let us come
to dream and to feel the water
forever trickling, going if it must
underground, but always arriving
to join its body in full.
Become as lake, accepting
waterfall, river and rain
and snow and ice
when they're tired of binding.
The trout and the stickleback
swim through us
beating their tiny fins
and coyotes, foxes, moose, and plovers
pause at our edges to drink.
There is only the blossoming wind
to shape and reshape our surfaces;
always we return through rise and fall
to the great unbreakable pool
of being, and are ever calm.
A shadow today, a sudden cloud—
what passes over
is lower than sun
that runnels down with its own
swift current, light
both reflection and entry.

The Day I Almost Drowned

RON YEOMANS

It was a beautiful fall day in October, an excellent day for fishing. The air was warm, the day was sunny, the leaves were turning, and the fish were moving back into shallow waters after their sojourn in the depths during the hot days of summer.

I gathered my fishing tackle and my preteen son, Eric, and hooked my boat to the pickup. We headed for a nearby lake.

My favorite uncle taught me to fish at an early age and I have never lost enthusiasm for it. There is always a sense of the unknown: will I catch fish today? Will it be a really good fishing day? What will I see that I've never seen before? Whatever happens with the fishing, there is always the sense of being away from the usual activities of everyday life and being close to nature, of coming back into contact with something very basic and very vital—back to the roots of our very being.

I've always felt a special connection both to water and to fishing. Our bodies are made up, in large part, of water, and apparently evolved from water-based life forms. Somehow, being on the water or around water feels like "going home."

I had a fairly new boat and motor with tiller steering. The steering was done with a motor handle rather than a steering wheel. By turning a grip on the handle, speed could be increased or decreased. When I moved the handle to the right or left, the boat changed directions.

Eric and I launched the boat and motored across the lake to one of the coves to try our luck. This cove didn't seem to be productive, so I decided to move to another part of the lake. I sat in the back, steering, and Eric sat in the front of the boat. I started across the cove at full speed, when suddenly the handle jerked sideways in my hand. I pitched over the side of the boat. One moment I was sitting in my seat, and the next moment I was in the water.

I plunged below the surface, exactly how far and for how long I don't know. The color of the water was a vivid green, and I can close my eyes years later and see that color.

I had heard stories of people being thrown from boats and then being run over and killed by the pilotless boat, which would run in circles with no one to guide it. This thought went through my mind. Somehow, I didn't seem to experience any fear. A sense of calm settled over me as I made my way back to the surface, half expecting to be hit at any time by the moving boat or its propeller.

I surfaced to see the boat sitting almost still in the water, with a dripping, saucer-eyed Eric staring at me from the front of the boat. The first thought that hit me was, "Well, I guess God isn't through with me yet."

As I climbed into the boat, Eric told me he had also been thrown out, and that he had climbed back in while I was still under water. I also learned that I had bought a motor with a safety feature I wasn't even aware of: when the handle is released, a spring automatically brings the speed control back to idle.

Eric and I returned to the dock and changed into dry clothes, and I spent the rest of the day being thankful.

Several times in my life I have felt protected by a guardian angel, or perhaps a whole fleet of guardian angels, but never more so than on that day.

Some baptisms are loving and gentle, while others are sudden and harsh. This one certainly got my attention and kept it.

Swimming Upstream

CAROLE BOSTON WEATHERFORD

In 1961, at age five, I had my first swimming lessons. Camp Y-Ho-Wah used the pool at Baltimore's Druid Hill Park. To get there, we campers passed the abandoned "colored-only pool," paint peeling from the dilapidated wooden bathhouse—a painful relic of the Jim Crow era. While segregation persisted farther south, I first stuck my toes into an integrated park pool. It was frigid. I lost what little enthusiasm I had when I skinned my knee on the pool's concrete bottom.

Years later, I would divide my girlfriends into two groups: those who kept their heads above water to protect their hairdos and those who wouldn't even get their feet wet. What had they to fear?

In 1803, Igbo (pronounced E-bo) tribesmen aboard a slave ship were on the last leg of their journey from present-day Nigeria to the Sea Islands of Georgia. Before the ship reached its destination, the captives rebelled. Lining up behind a chieftain, the tribesmen chanted to their god, Chukwu, as they marched toward a mass drowning.

The ocean claimed countless African lives and bore millions into bondage, but the waters occasionally buoyed hope. For young Frederick Douglass, a slave at a Chesapeake Bay plantation, the water symbolized liberty. Douglass later worked in a Baltimore shipyard and, disguised as a sailor, fled slavery on a northbound train.

> *More often, runaways escaped on foot, eluding slave*
> *catchers. Fugitive slaves waded in streams and creeks to*
> *make their scent undetectable to hounds.*

A decade ago, the late Samuel Proctor, a prominent black Baptist clergyman, suggested that water could be the salvation of urban youth. He advocated swimming lessons for inner-city youngsters. Learning to swim, he reasoned, teaches youths to master their environment and makes the world their oyster. After all, earth is two-thirds water. That ratio beckons some and paralyzes others.

> *Though the Xhosa inhabited South Africa's coast*
> *for ages, the tribe—landlocked by superstition—built no*
> *crafts to navigate the waters and did not fish, believing*
> *monsters lurked in the deep.*

No such fear grounded my mother, who never learned to swim as a child growing up in a Southern town with a whites-only pool. She was past fifty when she and several friends from Hollywood bathing beauty Esther Williams's generation enlisted a gym teacher to give them swimming lessons. Each day after work they gathered at one lady's backyard pool and practiced the basics: blowing bubbles, holding their breath, floating, gliding, stroking, and finally, jumping feet-first into the deep end. My mother still takes pride in her accomplishment. "Watch me jump in!" she insists, as her grandchildren splash in the pool on our family farm.

The farm, which has been in our family since Reconstruction, is less than a mile from Wye House, the waterfront plantation where young Frederick Douglass watched boats pass. My father was raised on that farm and learned to dog paddle in a nearby creek. His grand-mother would not have approved, believing the murky waters were snake-infested.

My own children crab from the wooden bridge that spans the creek. I know it is only a matter of time before my son dives off that bridge into the brackish water. My son perfected his dive at age four, before he knew a lick about swimming or water safety. We were on the deck of an apartment complex pool. Due to risks and liability, there was no diving board, and a sign on the fence strictly forbade diving. Older boys broke the rules and dived off the edge. Over and over again, my son watched them until he mustered enough nerve to emulate their moves.

Without warning, he curled his back and rolled off the edge into the water. Had I been an Olympic judge, I would have given him a respectable score. As his mother, however, I was compelled to scold him.

My daughter is just as foolhardy. At the beach, she ventures farther and farther from shore. Facing the hori-zon, she disobeys my orders to go just knee-deep into the ocean, despite the fact that she nearly drowned one sum-mer. She and her father had been holding hands as they jumped waves at North Carolina's Outer Banks when a crashing wave loosened their grips and knocked her down. Had her father, who once witnessed a drowning, not lodged his size-twelve foot on her back until he could grasp her arm, she would have been caught in the undertow.

As an adult, I had a similar scare at Rehoboth Beach, Delaware. Toppled by a towering wave, I was at the ocean's mercy for what seemed like a breathless eternity. Though close to shore and a good swimmer, I may as well have been driftwood. As the African proverb says, "It is the expert swimmer whom the river carries away."

When I was a child, I was nowhere near as daring as my son and daughter. My first dive in a YWCA pool still makes me shudder. From a sitting position on the shallow end of the pool, I landed upside down, bumping my head on the bottom, my feet jutting out of the water. While chlorine assailed my nostrils, I struggled to turn myself right side up. That experience haunted me for years. Sure, I could float as far as I could hold my breath, but I dared not attempt a dive. Swimming was one of the most difficult skills I ever tried to master.

By the summer of 1968, I had all but given up on swimming. My father enrolled me in swimming lessons at Baltimore's Frederick Douglass High School, where he taught printing and headed the industrial arts department. The instructor drilled me over and over from the pool's deck. With a firm voice that echoed throughout the natatorium, he coaxed me to relax, arch my back, lean gently backward onto the water, extend my legs, and look behind me at the ceiling. He showed me how to turn my head and inhale and how to push the water by rotating my arms. "Imagine that your hands are bunches of bananas hitting the water," he suggested.

Lastly, he helped me synchronize breaths and strokes. With his encouragement, I mastered the forward crawl. Perhaps I would not have caught on so quickly had I known that the next lesson would be diving off the board into ten feet of water. The four or so feet between the board and the pool's surface gave me pause. I'd done enough bellyflops off the side of the pool to know the humiliating sting of a botched dive. But I tried anyway. What my dive lacked in grace, it made up for in guts.

I suppose there is something to be said for teaching African-American children to swim. But is swimming instruction imperative? Lee Pitts, a Birmingham, Alabama, swimming instructor and scuba diver, thinks so. His videotape "Waters: Beginner's Swim Lessons for Adults and Children with Lee Pitts" seeks to drown paranoia about deep water.

"Swimming is something that should be handed down from generation to generation," Pitts asserts. He views swimming as a survival skill, no less important than reading, writing, and arithmetic. Statistics underscore his point. African Americans drown at twice the rate of whites.

But that doesn't give anyone the right to say we're not buoyant. That stereotype simply doesn't hold water against the backdrop of African-American history. We've been swimming upstream and treading water for centuries. Though our boats were on the bottom, we somehow kept dreams afloat.

Cleansing

ANTHONY WOODLIEF

We baptized Caroline in the between years—older than the Presbyterians suggest, but much younger than the Baptists allow. She was two years old and our tardiness—or haste—was a consequence of our new faith.

There was trepidation the night before because Caroline was afraid of men with beards and didn't like getting water on her head, and the next morning our bearded pastor was going to drip water on her curly brown locks.

My wife and I grew up in the South, which means that we call our pastor "preacher." Caroline mispronounced this and called him the "creature." We explained what would happen the next day, and she didn't seem very enthusiastic about our plans. My wife prayed that God would speak to our daughter's spirit in the baptism, while I prayed that the child wouldn't squawk.

Midway through the next morning's service, we stood beside the pulpit, staring out at the crowd of gentle faces we had come to know in the preceding months. Caroline clung to me as her eyes, wide and innocent, surveyed first the congregation and then the creature. He went through the ceremony: Do you acknowledge that your child is a sinner in need of Christ's atonement? Yes. Do you promise to raise her in the teachings of the church? Yes. Then came the prayer and the water.

There was no crying. Instead, there were quiet gasps from the women in the front rows as they witnessed Caroline's face, which in that moment was so beautiful and peaceful that it seemed to reflect heaven itself. She smiled up at the creature, and he smiled back as he prayed a blessing on her head.

Afterward the women circled around and each asked the other if she had seen the angelic face. Each confirmed that she had, and the men looked on and nodded that they too had seen it, and wasn't it the most precious thing. It was as if she had known what was happening, they said, even though she was only two. Caroline no longer called the preacher "creature" after that. Instead, she called him God, at least for a time. He liked that.

That was Father's Day, 1998. A year and a month later the doctors diagnosed a tumor the size of an egg nestled like a viper against Caroline's brainstem. There would be no recovery, though some led us on with false hope in poisons, so that we nearly killed her with chemotherapy. Her body died slowly, along with her spirit, and through her, we learned how to die as well.

In the final weeks, when the tumor had twisted her foot, folded her arm to her chest, and clamped shut her teeth, warm baths were one of the few things that soothed her. My wife would fill the tub and get in, and then I would pick up Caroline gently, slowly, but never gentle and slow enough to prevent tears. I carried her like a beached fish to the water and eased her into it. She whimpered as I held her out from my body, until she felt her mother's belly beneath her. Then she lay there watching us, and we spoke softly to her and washed her as tenderly as we could.

When we finished, I lifted her carefully as she moaned, swaddled her in a towel, and carried her to our bed. There we rubbed lotion into her skin, and my wife prayed over her for so very long, and I watched and quietly seethed at God for letting this happen, begging Him to let me be crippled and dying instead.

One night Caroline went into a coma, and two days later she died. She sweated as the tumor worked its final havoc on her compressed brainstem, and her hair—what little remained from the chemotherapy—matted itself to her tortured brow.

In the moments when life left her, she sighed and her eyelids fluttered as she tried to open them but couldn't. My wife cried out in a panicked voice that these were her final breaths, and I leaned close to her, so that my mouth was on her ear, and I whispered, "Go with Jesus, sweetheart. Mommy and Daddy will be there soon."

As if in obedience, she breathed out once again, a long sigh, and then she breathed no more. We wept and held her, and then we laid out her body on our bed. I put warm water and baby soap in a wash pan, and we bathed Caroline a final time. Her limbs moved freely; the tumor had no hold on her in death. We cleaned her sweet face—swollen from steroids, but without the contortion now—then her neck, her thin arms, her bloated torso. Only her toes and ears were the same as they had always been: soft and beautiful, like a little girl's should be. We washed all of her, and we rinsed her in fresh, clean water.

Looking back on those moments, I think this last bath was for our souls, just as the baptism was for hers. We desperately needed to feel her as she had been—to hold her fingers, though they dropped limply from our grasp, to run hands over her skin without hearing a groan of pain in reply, to squeeze her without feeling the resistance of her twisted little limbs. We cleansed the stink of death from her there on our bed, though we could not break its hold on her body, on our hearts. It still lingers in mine like a poison, and I don't know what water will wash it away.

I've thought a lot these last four years about what it meant for me, a dark-hearted man, to be responsible for cleansing this pure-hearted little girl. I gave Caroline her first bath in this world, sponging away the blood and fluid of birth. I held her during the baptism, her symbolic bathing in Christ's blood, when she was cleansed from theoretical sins in a future she did not have. And with this last bath, I washed the freshness of death from her just as I had washed the freshness of life.

I remember all of these cleansings so clearly. I remember, and I wonder if I have ever been that clean, and if I ever will be, and why someone like me ever had the right to cleanse someone so innocent. Only living water can bear so heavy a burden, to be wielded by the impure so that it intercedes for the near-innocent, to clean away imperfect life and immutable death. Drink of this water, a wandering man told the Samaritan woman, and you will thirst no more.

I believe Caroline thirsts no more. But sometimes I am so parched. Can the water soothe this bitterness in my throat? Do I really believe the words I whispered to my daughter as she breathed her last in this world?

Perhaps the dying faith of this country is related to our forgetting the sacred place water holds in creation. We turn a knob and it pours out. We spray it over our lawns, hose it across our SUVs, pipe it up from fountains that decorate our megamalls, all without thought to the sacred that lingers around us.

The sacred is diminished now because we are diminished, because we have forgotten that holy means separate, and because we have refused to separate ourselves from our daily pleasures to consider that there is power in the water. It is the power of life and redemption—I know because I have seen it in Caroline's smile.

Benediction

SUSAN CARMAN

Sunlight streams
through the church window,
illuminates our family tableau
before the marble font. Above us
hovers a stained glass dove, wings unfurled.

"Name this child," the priest says,
my infant son cradled in his arms.
He christens him in the names
of our fathers, sprinkles his head
with water infused with the breath
of the Spirit. Soft as a sigh,
the blessing settles on him.

I feel Jordan's banks beneath my feet,
hear familiar words, *"This is my Son,*
in whom I am well pleased."
I gather my child in my arms,
inhale his fragrant innocence,
touch my lips to his forehead,
damp with liquid benediction.

Running Water Pushing Sand

DIANE SIMS

Thousands of years ago, the Batchawana River deposited sand, grit, and wood shavings downstream. This running water created an island and lent its name to a ten-mile stretch of bay along the north shore of Lake Superior, providing protection from the lake's raw wind and waves.

Batchawana is an Ojibwa term meaning "running water pushing sand." That running water taught me respect for the water, my father, and life itself.

I spent childhood summers at the family cottage tucked safely into the bay. My father was a captain on the Great Lakes. We had a fleet of old runabouts with make-and-break engines riding the waves. I learned to bail a boat before I learned to read.

I doubt my father ever bought a boat. Many were given in appreciation and some were given to refurbish. As a child, I loved diving to count the number of anchors, cement blocks, and chains.

I was eight when my father taught me to start engines; tie knots; identify ship horns, smokestacks, and lengths; and read charts.

By ten, I thought myself invincible on the water.

One morning in late July, I proudly churned into the bay at the helm of a fourteen-foot, square bow steel boat, shallow stern heavy with the nine-horsepower Evinrude engine. Proud that the *Minnow* could not tip, I learned she could swamp.

I headed to the "gap"—the narrow, fast-running channel between the land and the island into the big water of Superior. Far out, I could not come-about without flooding the stern.

Cold and frightened, my face was wet with tears and spray. No one on land would see me. I cut the engine to almost neutral, moved closer to the bow to distribute my weight, and tried using an oar to bring her about.

Neither the boat nor the water responded. Large boulders from a retreating glacier surrounded the island, warning off foolish boaters.

If I swamped or ran the boat onto a boulder, I knew I didn't have the strength to fight the pace of the rushing, running water.

Then I saw the wash of a speedboat. I was drawing more water, couldn't bail fast enough, and couldn't row the heavy hull. I waved my oar. She cut her engine, slowly coming alongside. I saw my neighbor and my father. Once alongside, I held the oar for my Dad to grasp. I was safe.

He had lost sight of me in the bay through his binoculars, knew the east wind boded ill, and feared I had gone outside the gap. (Gap-crashing was a favorite family pastime, but always with my father at the helm. The sound and pounding of hitting wave after wave was exhilarating!)

Once outside the gap, my father saw my red hair and the *Minnow*'s yellow bow through his well-traveled World War II binoculars.

My father took the *Minnow*'s helm and headed into the waves with confidence, despite that steel boat holding even more water. I bailed the two bow sections with my arms aching. Gradually, Dad made a very long tack.

Our neighbor kept abreast and we finally passed back through the channel. Dad waved the neighbor off and cut our engine to slow. He tossed me a soaked Crispy Crunch bar and opened one for himself.

We ate in silence. I looked everywhere but at him.

Finally, he said, "Diane, what have you learned?"

"Not to go outside the gap alone."

"No," he replied, "not at all."

Surprised, I glanced his way.

"You must always check the direction of the wind and then go against it wherever you are. Check your speed and always keep watch astern. OK?"

I was diagnosed with multiple sclerosis at seventeen. The doctors told me I would be bedridden by the time I was twenty-seven, and dead by the time I was thirty-five.

Well, I went against the wind and waves of that diagnosis.

I went dancing on an all-night pub crawl when I was twenty-seven, and have lived past thirty-five. Somewhere in those years Dad's binoculars were stolen. He made it through World War II and beyond with those glasses. I remain sad that they were stolen from the cottage and waters he loved so much.

My father died when I had just turned twenty.

My only sister, Karen, died of cancer when I was thirty-seven. Four months later, our mom died, and four months after that I was diagnosed with the same cancer as Karen. I was given less than a year to live. I have had eight surgeries and I am headed for four more. I am forty-five. I have fought against this cancer, always remembering my father's words and what the water taught me that day.

I steer toward the surgeries with my hand at the helm, directing my energy to life, but keeping watch of the ill east winds behind me.

I hope my father knows how valuable that day remains. He taught me about rough, running waters and pushing sand.

So I run on, and I will push on, until my ashes are sprinkled over those waters that taught me such a sacred lesson.

Waterwoman

HARRIET SMITH

Like many people, I have always been attracted to water. But nothing prepared me for my obsessive love of working on the water as a commercial fisherman. "Obsessive" is the right word—it is an addiction. A spell of bad weather or boat repairs will cause a fisherman to start pacing the floor.

On the water, there are no phones, no bills, no traffic. Just you and the boat and Mother Nature. You hope that you can be smart enough and lucky enough to be in the right place at the right time to catch your share. In the meantime, you hope you won't tear a hole in your boat or have a motor breakdown.

It is the most basic of activities and, at the same time, the most complicated. I won't say, "You against Mother Nature," because if you are "against" Mother Nature, you will always lose. You work with her, and sometimes, she will let you have your catch and not snare you with lightning or stingrays or water too shallow.

Yes, there are large boats, instruments, spotter planes, power winches, and five-mile driftnets. But you are still a frail human on the mighty ocean with only your skill and luck to serve you.

If you travel the world, you will see the same nets being cast and fishermen in late morning back on shore selling their catch.

I watched one fisherman in a little town on the Pacific Coast of Nicaragua as he finished his work for the day. He came into shore and unloaded his catch to waiting buyers, including villagers who came with buckets to buy a fish or two. Then, he pushed away from the shore and tied the boat to a buoy—not an easy task with good-sized swells.

After cleaning the boat, he unplugged the gas tank, put on his shirt, and jumped overboard with the gas tank. He swam to shore, pushing the floating tank ahead of him, and walked home with it on his shoulder. Catching fish is not so different anywhere on earth.

What *is* different is in our country: pollution, coastal development, faster and noisier boats, the depletion of fish stocks, and incredibly poor fish management. In Florida, where I used to live, the State banned the use of gill nets to catch fish. With the stroke of a pen, commercial fishing was forever changed.

The "net ban," as it was called, was an amendment to the Florida Constitution put forward by a lobbying group of sport fishermen. Voters, ignorant of the fact that 6,000 small subsistence fishermen made up the bulk of those affected, voted in favor of the amendment, not understanding that the net size would be so restrictive that it would be impossible to use effectively. What voters then found was that, except for the fish caught by the offshore deepwater fishermen, the fish they put on their table was imported.

Usually, I fished for "jimmies" or Atlantic Spot. Just about the best day of my fishing life was when Mike, who managed the local fish house, said, "She's a pretty fair jimmy fisherman." This was high praise indeed. But the fishing adventures ended with the ban on gill nets.

I stood at the fish house as the last basket of mullet was hauled up and tried, like the men around me, not to cry.

We turned to the only thing we could—clam farming. Through a job-training program, we each leased four acres of submerged land from the State of Florida.

The work consisted of counting and measuring baby clams—each about 10 millimeters across—into a four-by-four-foot nylon mesh bag. I planted the bags on the bottom of the submerged land, staking the bags down in rows, just like planting corn. The only difference was, I couldn't see anything. I called it "farming by Braille" because I could only feel with my feet and hands what was going on.

After a year, I harvested from five to forty bags out of the mud and sand, brought them to shore, put them in my truck, and took them to a clam buyer.

Each time I worked my clam lease, I was in the water. This water, with its magical invisible life, could be smooth as silk, could smell like morning freshness, or could push wave after wave into my face as I tried to work.

Depending on the tide and time of year, sometimes I worked in water that lapped at my ankles, and sometimes the water sloshed up to my armpits, and I had to duck and dive to do my work.

These were some of my happiest days. I knew the water; I loved and respected it. The clean, cool air of the Gulf at sunrise or the pink and gold sunset sky; the feel of the water as I lowered myself into it and became part of it; thousands of days of sun and sky and salt and water of different feel, different height, and different temperature. It became a second home to me.

I worked my clam lease for several years until the lifting and pulling of the heavy bags was physically too difficult. I sold my lease. Six months went by and I had not put my boat into the water.

How could this happen? I loved the water so much. It was the best thing I had ever done, and I loved it. But it was time to move on.

Now I live on the side of a volcano in Costa Rica, raising cows, volunteering in a rainforest. I look for adventures whenever they come my way, choose the ferry instead of the bridge, and the boat ride instead of the bus ride. One more thing: I'm drawing plans for a small wooden boat to take me up the San Juan River into Nicaragua.

10,000 Islands

ART RITAS

I felt the power of my stroke carry me over the swells. A novice kayaker, I was a little smug about how well I was keeping up with my more experienced partners, Don and Jim.

On the beach at Rabbit Key, we got out of our boats and stood together, silent. We looked back at the expanse of rolling, rough water over which we'd come to the northernmost region of the Florida Gulf Coast's 10,000 Islands. I gripped the graphite shaft of my paddle and felt superior again. Man over nature.

We opened the hatches and pulled out the gear: tents, sleeping bags, pads, stoves, food, and all the other things to ensure our comfort. Somewhere in the back of my mind was a thought—this stuff is actually necessary to our survival.

Jim scouted the beach for campsites. "We can pitch two right here," he said, pointing to a sandy clearing just above the debris of a high water mark. I looked to even higher ground and remnants of the raccoons' meals: perforated conch shells and overturned horseshoe crabs, the innards pulverized. I didn't want to be too close to where the raccoons took their meals, so I took a few steps toward the Gulf.

"We'll set up here," I shouted to Don, who was

smoothing out an elevated site down the beach. I threw down my ground cloth, feeling relieved, then expansive. *This is my home for the night. I am just like any other animal marking a spot to defend. I am sooo . . . centered.*

Jim was already two steps ahead of me. He had his tent poles through their nylon sleeves, and he was about to erect his little igloo dome. Kayaks and igloos. Ah, wilderness. Ah, men together in the wild. I could feel myself straightening up, my lungs filling. *Me, a big man. A paddler and camper, alone in the wild, almost.*

Soon we had a respectable-looking campsite. We were in our tripod chairs sitting around a fire of red and black mangrove logs gathered from the beach.

"This is it," Jim said.

"Too bad most people don't have the guts to come out here. They'll never see this," Don said, looking out over the red glow at the advancing waters.

Across the way white ibis were streaming onto a rookery island, necks extended, black wingtips beating. The brown pelicans had already snuggled in. I turned to the fire and stretched out my legs. I could feel the heat on my bare toes . . . and the cold at my back. I knew we were headed for the low 40s that night. Frigid for south Florida.

Dinner was a simple affair. Open a pouch; pour in boiling water; close pouch; wait ten minutes; open pouch; spoon "chicken teriyaki" into mouth. Camp cuisine.

"That was better than you'd expect," Don said, folding his empty foil bag neatly and putting it into our trash receptacle, an old, yellow mesh grapefruit bag. We stowed all the food and garbage in Jim's boat, secured the hatch, and lifted my boat on top.

"Raccoon proof," Jim said. I wondered if two strong raccoons could knock my boat off Jim's and chew through the hatch, our water bags, and our freeze-dried dinners. I'd heard stories.

We made the campsite shipshape. I took a last look at the musical stars in the unfamiliar heavens and crawled on all fours into my tent. Soon I was buried deep in my bag, a blanket thrown over my head, listening to Jim sawing wood. I heard the alternating rhythms: Jim . . . then the gentle lapping of the water. Harsh, then smooth. Beautiful contrast, dissonant noises in the starry night. And me, complacent body, settled in against the cold.

I was cocooned, on the edge of sleep. *How perfectly I have fit myself into this wilderness, the greatest east of the Mississippi.* Then I heard the too-loud whisper. It drowned out Jim's snoring. I felt a disturbance, a warning deep inside me.

I squiggled out of the bag, stood in a crouch, unzipped the tent door, and took a look at what I'd been hearing. The tide was lapping with a gentle insistence a foot from my threshold, closer with each shushing sound.

I'd have to wake Jim; we'd have to scramble to clear away the brush on higher ground; we'd have to drag our stuff out of the tents and get everything up beyond the reach of the tide.

Before I called out to him, I stopped to listen to the water beckoning. I felt the synchronized rhythm, the push and the release.

For a few seconds, I was small again. *How will it feel to stop protecting and inflating myself? Where am I headed? Why am I here?*

Swallowed by something bigger but unafraid, I wanted—during these seconds before I called out to Jim—to be embraced and swept away.

Monsoon Blessings

AMMINI RAMACHANDRAN

"What is monsoon like in your hometown?" asked my American friends as we were leaving the theater after seeing the Indian movie *Monsoon Wedding*. For a moment, I was lost for words as memories flooded in.

Was it waking at dawn to the sounds of rainwater gushing through the drains into the central courtyard? Was it the delicate fragrance of sandalwood incense sticks mingled with the strong scent of lighted camphor cubes that came from our prayer room where my mother paid homage to the goddess of plenty?

Was it the first shower through which I trekked my way to school and back, with overturned umbrella and dripping wet skirt? Was it the surprise of looking out of school windows and wondering why it was not raining then, but would be pouring again when we left school? Was it the fun we had in the evenings making paper boats with old newspapers and floating them in the water-drenched backyard? Was it enjoying a bowl of warm *kanji* (rice soup) dotted with dollops of golden *ghee* (clarified butter) at supper while monsoon rains fell relentlessly?

The arrival of monsoon clouds over the Arabian Sea is an eagerly awaited event in my home state of Kerala, in southwest India. The muggy air seems to bear down upon everyone. After a dry spell, lasting for months on end, the parched earth calls out for the first drop of rain. Sun and even the red earth give off endless heat. Then, one day, the unbearable wait comes to an end. Accompanied by howling winds and rumbling thunder, torrential rains break a lengthy spell of scorching temperatures.

Our monsoon is no ordinary heavy shower. It is magical, it is romantic, it is divine, and above all, it is our lifeline. Gusts of wind blow away everything in their path. The tranquil sea becomes a turbulent pool of water. Loud thunder, bright streaks of lightning, blowing winds, and swaying palms add to the spectacle.

The most spectacular clouds and rain occur against the Sahyaadri Mountain ranges (Western Ghats), where the early monsoonal airstream piles up against the steep slopes, then recedes, then piles up again to a greater height. Each time it pushes thicker clouds upward until wind and clouds roll over the barrier and, after a few brief spells of absorption by the dry inland air, cascade toward the interior. Monsoon mornings bring an invigorating smell of damp earth, budding leaves, washed streets, knee-deep water, crisp air, and ominous clouds rolling across the sky.

But monsoon is also about cleansing, regeneration. When the first raindrops fall, it is almost as if the land and its creatures heave a collective sigh of relief. With the monsoon comes a renewal of the life cycle of farming, a gift from God. In subtropical India, planting and harvesting are largely dependent on seasons. Cultivation begins with the onset of rainy season. Once the seedlings are planted, they need more water to ensure a good harvest. Rainfall is crucial to the cultivation of rice and a drought means famine. This climatic shift is considered nothing less than a holy event, and the arrival of monsoon is welcomed with many rituals and ceremonies.

At the onset of monsoon season we welcome Sridevi, the goddess of plenty and prosperity. Houses get a thorough cleaning. Floors are scrubbed and mopped, cobwebs cleaned, and furniture dusted.

Toward dusk of the first day of monsoon season each year, one of our maidservants, a pail of trash in hand, would walk out of our front door. We children accompanied her, shouting *chetta purathu poo, Sridevi akathuva*—let all the dirt and evil go out the door and let cleanliness and goodness come inside. My mother walked behind her sprinkling handfuls of water on the floor: water, the eternal purifier.

From the next day on, we set up a special place in our prayer room to honor the goddess. My mother decorated a wooden plank symbolizing the goddess with sandalwood paste, bright red *kumkumam* powder, and garlands of seasonal yellow *mukkutti* flowers and dark green *karuka* grass.

Among the lighted bronze oil lamps and platters of fruits and flowers rested a silver bowl filled with fresh water drawn from our well—*theertham*, nurturing sacred water, the spiritual source of life. A lone holy basil leaf would be floating in it.

Mother sprinkled this water on fruits and *nivedyam*, a bowl of popped rice mixed with fresh coconut and brown sugar, to propitiate the goddess. After our morning baths, we entered the prayer room with cupped right palms to receive a spoonful of this sacred water. Then we got a small serving of delicious *nivedyam* offered to the goddess.

Now life continues here in the United States, with memories of those rain-filled days of *Edavapathi*, the southwestern monsoon, and what it means to me to have been born in a land blessed with the power of water.

The Spilling Jar

DHAKA STATION, BANGLADESH

JUNE OWENS

Gray is everywhere. Station walls,
concrete floors. Columns. Sky
gone zinc with it. The air also.
We two women wait. We notice
each other, pretend we do not.
She is brown. I am white.
I feel the power of her concentration:
she senses an imminence.
I say: what is your name?
She turns away. Only a little,
smiling, eyes down. I ask again.
Shalini, she says. Alice, say I.
She moves to platform edge, carries
a black earthen jar, a metal basin.

Rain does not rain in Bangladesh.
It batters. Sudden. Solid. Slanting.
As though shot from slings.
We are soaked in its silver,
feel its shafts go not around
but through us. Clothes cling.
Her sari, my skirt and blouse.
We laugh at ourselves.
Far off, egrets rise.
I see her small, bright teeth.
She is beautiful. Thin.
Unshapely, yet correctly formed.
A face like forever.

Rain changes her to glaze. Glaze
goes ceramic, caught in a figurine
moment. Only the great black jar
she fills with pounding water
is darker than she.

I ask if I may help her lift
the spilling jar.
No. No. It is *my* part, she says.
My part alone. No. It is
quite improper to burden
a new water friend.

Water Princess

JULIE ANN SHAPIRO

Water is the drink of my soul, teaching me secrets and giving me a place to dream. I hear the pounding of the surf every day, running by the ocean. The churning water takes me back in time to water memories, the ones that have seeped into my soul.

I can still see the copper penny my first swimming instructor put at the bottom of the pool, glowing in the sunlight, the squares of light like a woven quilt fluttering across the water's surface. I arched my body, held my breath, dived into the cool, crisp water, and reached down, feeling the hard surface of the penny against my fingers. Instead of picking it up, I kicked hard on the bottom of the swimming pool, propelling my body upwards. On the surface, I took a deep breath, then kicked my arms and legs hard, back and forth, stopping and gliding, continuing over and over again, until my strokes became reflexes and my arms and legs felt as though they were made of water. In the background, I heard my mother say, "Look at her go, she's like a fish," but that day I was a mermaid. A part of me still is.

I remember the childhood games of Marco Polo, that water-bound hide-and-seek game, and how on one particular day I was chosen to find my friends with my eyes closed. At first, I tried finding them in one direction and then the next, but eventually gave up, choosing instead to float on my back and stomach and listen to the muffled sounds of the outside world growing fainter and fainter.

A friend yelled, "Are you playing or not?" Of course I was, I'd just found a new game—floating in a world without sight—and I was brave. I dived down toward the bottom, where the world grew quiet, and I wasn't afraid to touch the bottom with just my arms to guide me. I was safe floating in the dark, feeling a lightness I'd never felt with my eyes open. In that world, in the darkness, there were colors without colors. I felt them. Deep blue was cold, and in the hot spots the color was red. In between, I found my castle, the world of dreams.

When I surfaced, I opened my eyes and folded my hair on the top of my head. I told my friends we were all water princesses.

Those memories echo now. Each time I float in a swimming pool, wade in the tide, or take a bath, I still see myself as a water princess, but also a princess who has learned the power of the sea and its danger.

On day three of my attempt to master the art of standing on water via the illustrious surfboard, amidst a fit of giggles with a friend and my husband, a big wave came. I paddled with the laugh still in my belly. The board conked me on the head. Red spurted from my face, mixing with the blue and white water.

I swam. The blue water and sky turned around and around, so many shades of blue swirled around me. My husband scooped me into his arms.

I felt the warm sand beneath me, and the cold water flowing over my nose and mouth as he flushed the blood. I watched the red water float out to sea, telling my listeners how it went from red to rust, and remarking how the sky and sea looked the same, all spinning around me.

They said, "You're delirious," and ran tests on me, trying to make sure I didn't have a concussion. "Of course I see the colors," I told them. "I'm a writer."

Water in the form of ice became my friend over the next few days. "A fractured nose," the doctor said, a typical surf injury, I proudly learned. But it was the end of my surfing days. I realized I'd never wanted to stand on water. I just wanted to float and dream: that's what mermaids and water princesses do.

The Stirring

Barbara A. Gates

The speed of my descent was alarming. A moment before, I had been standing in an inch of seawater, the vestige of a previous wave that blanketed the sand. Then my feet were jerked from under me, and I fell to my hands and knees, sliding swiftly downward toward the next gaping wave.

Water, thrill me.

I was twelve. My mother tried to grab my hair as I passed her, but the thin sheet of water ripped me from her grasp. With my hands and knees immobilized by the ocean, I had no ability or time to struggle. Within a couple of stunning seconds, I had been swallowed by the ocean, out of my family's view.

I entered a different world. The seabed was inclined so steeply that I could see neither sand nor sky in my watery cocoon. As I was pulled farther out, the water began to roll my body into a slow spin, feet first, heels over head.

I watched my legs among the ocean debris as I turned somersaults in slow motion. The movement of the roiling water was so powerful that there was no hope of resistance. I waited to drown.

Still unable to see anything but slow moving water, I kept my eyes open and entered a dream-like state of suspension. I felt cradled by a power vastly greater than myself. Eyes open in wonderment, still holding my breath, I was at peace, enveloped and gently tumbled as if by loving arms.

Water, cradle me.

Time stopped as I rolled over and over. Then, sand met my feet at an unexpected, awkward angle. I struggled for equilibrium as my feet tried to make sense of gravity and the steep slope of sand.

Hauling myself up on unsteady legs—like a baby standing for the first time—I discovered that I was facing the land and a group of horrified onlookers. I was waist deep in water that pulled me backward; I could not move toward land.

Understanding that their shouts were lost in the roar of the ocean, the people began pointing insistently—not at me but higher above my head. I looked over my shoulder in confusion, just in time to take a breath as a huge wave broke over my head and tumbled me like a twig.

Water, release me.

The force of the wave tossed me toward the shore, where two men waded in and tugged me out before I was sucked under again. One on each arm, they dragged me to a beach towel and lowered me to the ground. I lay, dazed and depleted, unable even to lift my head.

Since then, water has held wonder and mystery for me. I respect its power. It had almost claimed my life, as it has claimed so many others'. When I moved away from the ocean, I cherished the rain. Now that I am in a drier climate, I gravitate to streams that swell when the Rocky Mountain snows melt in the spring.

Water, sustain me.

I learned that facing death was not as terrifying as I had expected. The intimacy and comfort of that admittedly horrendous experience still captivate me. In midlife, I began working as a chaplain, helping others work through issues surrounding illness and death. I attended seminary and became a minister—not to proselytize or pastor, but to continue on my own spiritual journey, of which this was an integral part.

Through my care of patients, I sat with people and dried their tears—and sometimes my own as well. When a young mother was severely injured in a car accident and suffered a miscarriage while she was unconscious, I stood beside her inert body in the ICU. She was on life support as I baptized her miscarried child. This little one joined the other deceased infants in my memory, whose families I cared for, whose tiny heads with closed eyes received water from my hand.

Water, welcome us.

Some of my most reflective moments are when I am at the ocean or beside a brook, gazing at the water and learning the rhythm of its unique voice. When I am overwhelmed by responsibilities, I go to water to heal. Water: the substance of my birth, the near cause of my death, the welcome of countless children into their family of faith, an ongoing symbol of life and joy.

Water, heal us.

Through water we are connected—not only to our water-rich bodies, but also to the earth and to one another. Water connects continents and peoples. The same ocean that almost took my life may have swept over a shark's streamlined body. It may have churned over an African boy's toes or held a ship aloft in a storm.

Water, unite us.

Water can mean life or death to us, but without it, we surely die. It can bring thirst-quenching relief . . .

or unbearable pain. I know a man who lost his young wife and both babies in a flash flood. He could not reach them; in an instant they were gone. Water sweeps over land in a rushing frenzy. Water also caresses stones in a streambed until they are smooth and glassy. I imagine some similarities with God, who overwhelms us at times, who also runs healing hands over our raw edges and gently smoothes them.

Water, refine us.

I continue to integrate that formative experience long ago of being cradled in water—those moments when I was not yet panicked by having to breathe fluid into my lungs. I remember the otherworldly experience of buoyancy, grace, and movement, with cushioning water around me. In that womb-like world, I discovered a profound comfort and assurance that has endured and continues to draw me ever deeper into the source of life and love.

Water, guide us.

Meditation:

WATER CEREMONIES—A FEW IDEAS

The ways in which water can be used ceremonially are as infinite as water itself. Many Native American traditions include water in praying to the four directions, most often as a symbol for the West. There it represents the fluid, shifting shadows of the subconscious mind, the emotions, and also calls forth all creatures of the sea.

Water's life-giving qualities are revered in every culture. Baptism rituals are a familiar ceremony in some religions. Baptism usually implies a rebirth or "new life," and water provides an appropriate medium for this transformation.

The many forms of baptism include everything from sprinkling water on the crown of the head to total immersion. Some religions offer a form of baptism ("christening") for infants, while others limit baptism to older children and adults. Ancient religions that worship water gods or goddesses have baptism or initiation rituals in rivers, creeks, and oceans.

In recent years, pregnant women have chosen to give birth in water, or with the help of water. Birthing rituals and ceremonies have sprung up to give power and sustenance to this form of delivery. Birthing in water reflects the fact that we are surrounded by fluid for the first nine months of our lives.

Water can also represent the abundance that comes with fertile fields and well-watered crops—and many sons and daughters to tend them.

I've participated in three contemporary water rituals that held great meaning. One was a small wedding ceremony, in which guests offered a spoken blessing to the couple while pouring a glass of water into a large crystal bowl. The wedding officiate spoke of how the mingled waters of friends and family would help to preserve and strengthen the marriage. The couple poured some of the water into two goblets and drank from them. After the ceremony, the couple took the water home as a visible reminder of all the blessings they had received, and used it to water their garden.

The second water ceremony involved grieving. The ritual leader set a large bowl of water in the midst of a circle of women. The water symbolized the tears of our sisters everywhere, and the loss of life and dignity women experience through being treated as less than equal, or being actually enslaved. The leader invited the women in the circle to come, one by one, and sit next to the bowl, speaking (aloud or silently) words of solidarity and support to their sisters across the globe. As women sat, many added their own tears to those already in the bowl.

The third water ceremony concluded a mediation between divorced parents who had joint custody of their daughter, but who had conflicting views of parenting, based on their vastly different cultural backgrounds. As the parents worked to understand each other, I pointed out that they each had cultural gifts to give to their child, and encouraged them to shift perspectives so that the child could benefit from both heritages.

When we reached an agreement, I took a simple pottery bowl, filled it with water, and had them each place a hand in the bowl. I told them that the water represented their child, and their hands—one from Nigeria and one from the United States—represented the gifts of each parent, separate and distinct, yet mingled in the water.

Some of the stories in this book feature water ceremonies and rituals. Use water whenever you want to create sacred space for yourself or others, or when you want to create connection with nature, with "flow," or with a higher purpose.

You can create your own ceremonies by asking: (1) What is the purpose or goal of this ceremony? (2) How will water enhance or promote the purpose? (3) What form of water will be best for the purpose I have in mind? When you have answered these questions clearly, the ways in which you can use water will also be clear.

Part Three

Water Legacies:
Stories of
Sacred Water Sites

Wade in the Water

MARIL CRABTREE

The day is hot and still. Along with a small group of spiritual pilgrims, I have flown to Brazil and traveled to the village of Abadiania, where we've spent a week at a healing center known as *Casa de Dom Ignacio* (the House of St. Ignatius). Being in Brazil is an opportunity to immerse myself in the energies of a different part of the world. It is November, near the height of the Brazilian summer. Villagers move slowly and easily through the days, reminding me that time is relative to culture and place. At night, the Southern Cross dominates a sky full of strange constellations.

Now, our leader tells us that we have a special treat. A mile down the dusty road behind the Casa lies a waterfall, considered sacred by those who come here to bathe. Certain days of the week are designated as "women only" and "men only" so that, if they desire, everyone can fully experience the waterfall without a swimsuit.

Ten of us women walk into the rocky hills behind the Casa, working up a good sweat as we toil up and down the hills. We've been warned that the waterfall will be cold, and right now, I can think of nothing that will feel better.

Finally, we leave the road and follow a gentle path into a thick grove of trees. I hear the rushing of water in the distance. We walk a little farther before our guide stops and points ahead. There, gushing over the side of a rocky ledge, is our waterfall, a sheer curtain of water about ten feet high, flowing into a stone-filled creek. To reach the waterfall we must step onto these stones, climbing as we go.

Laughing, we shed our clothes and help each other clamber up the stones. Our leader calls for silence. Quietly and reverently, she addresses the four directions, acknowledges the presence of our ancestors, and asks the blessing of all beings. One by one, she invites us to cleanse and purify ourselves, to heal our wounds—physical, mental, emotional, or spiritual—with this sacred, life-giving water.

I plunge into the icy curtain, kneeling on the stone beneath it, letting the needle-sharp force pour over me from head to toe. Images of other baptismal experiences rush over me, along with the water: I am ten years old, swinging from a rope to drop into the swimming hole near my grandmother's place in the country, feeling that unique combination of fear and thrill as I fling myself through the air. I am twelve, kneeling with others on Palm Sunday while the minister anoints us with water "in the name of the Father, the Son, and the Holy Spirit." I am forty, standing waist-deep in a natural hot springs beside the Rio Grande on a starry solstice night, then submersing myself completely as I become one with everything around me.

The frigid water spilling over me jolts me back to the present. I feel myself filling up with joy, laughter, and love for all of us brave pilgrims who have traveled halfway around the world in search of healing. Standing naked under an icy waterfall is its own form of healing, and I imagine my soul's weary wounds closing, along with my pores, clearing the way for a fresh start.

It is good to be in this place of sacred water. Whether our wounds are visible or invisible, it is good to have places where they can be acknowledged, honored, cleansed, and healed. I am glad to live in a world where we honor one another's wounds, where we play each other's sacred tunes to create a symphony of understanding, where we kneel before a mystery as ancient and everlasting as this sacred waterfall.

The Song at the Well

SUSAN ELIZABETH HALE

It is April, a month which means "to open" in Celtic. All the buds have opened, and spring lambs leap in the gently rolling hills of Somerset in southern England. I am at Chalice Well Gardens in Glastonbury with four women from New York City, leading a Grail Quest. We are here to learn the ancient myths that surround this unusual town and to sing to its many sacred sites.

The Holy Grail is said to reside at the bottom of Chalice Well. We have come here to address personal and collective wounds, and to experience its powerful healing waters. I have come here to seek further healing from recent news of my father's death.

We begin the first evening with a ritual at the well, washing away our pilgrim dust from trains and airplanes, and drinking from its waters. A chant emerges: "Drink from the well, drink from her waters, rest and be well." We tie white ribbons on the yew trees to represent our intentions. With few people in the garden we feel free to sing to the well, to nourish it in return for the healing it brings us.

After our personal ritual, we become part of a larger ceremony. A Tibetan lama blesses the well with his deep-voiced chant, along with holy water and herbs. I can imagine no place as peaceful and healing to both body and soul as Chalice Well. The gardens are in their first bloom. Bluebells, jonquils, and tulips of every color line the tranquil paths. The birds are a constant voice guarding their new nests. One woman from the group tells us that what has been missing from her life is the sound of the water in the well. She has been searching for this sound.

One of our guides, author Nicholas Mann, speaks to us of Avalon as the inner world of Glastonbury, a place that is both now and ancient. Avalon is called many things: the Land of the Blessed, the Land of Apples, the Land Under the Waves, the Land of Women, the Land of the Dead, and the Land of the Living. It is the legendary resting place of King Arthur in the Western Isle of the Dead, a place where souls are reborn. To enter Avalon one must part the veil to see into the Otherworld. The mists of Avalon part to reveal a magical world that lies within the enchanted landscape of Glastonbury.

Avalon is the place of souls. According to legend, a woman carrying a silver apple branch meets the newly dead. They go to a place where birds sing all day and all night. The souls are taken on Samhaim, our Halloween, to the underworld home of Gwynn ap Nudd, the White Son of Night, King of the Fairy Folk. Here they feast and make love until they are ready for rebirth. "The purpose of incarnation was to incarnate as everything," said Nicholas. "The dead may be reborn as the song of a bird, a bud on a tree, a light on a wave, or the voice of a poet."

As Nicholas spoke these words, I thought of my father. Just before I left on this seven-week trip, my brother told me that if anything happened to either of our elderly parents, who shared a room together in a nursing home, he would arrange for an immediate cremation and a delayed memorial service when I returned.

My father, whose memory had been erased by Alzheimer's, had died of pneumonia, water filling his lungs a few days before his eighty-second birthday. I received news of his death when I was teaching at a voice conference in Wales, and did a ceremony of release on the shores of the Irish Sea.

Now, as I listen to Nicholas's words, I gaze at the Holy Thorn decorated with colorful Easter eggs hanging from ribbons on the branches. Christian images of resurrection mingle with Celtic images of rebirth. I wonder whether my father is now the fragrance of the blossoms or the sound of water in the well.

Here in Glastonbury I am greeted with new words of how death becomes life. It is hard to be so far away on distant shores, yet it feels as if all has been arranged by a travel agent wearing angel's wings. Chalice Well Gardens, where tulips, bleeding hearts, and forget-me-nots spring from the earth, along with pansies, primroses, and daffodils, is the perfect place to stand in the veil between death and rebirth, the perfect place to remember my father, an avid gardener who had built a gazebo surrounded by roses in our backyard. He would have loved it here.

A gardener wearing green greets me and asks me how I am. My eyes well up with tears as I tell him about my father. I describe his sweet face, hazel eyes, white woolly hair, his corny jokes, quick wit, and easy laugh. The gardener smiles, hugs me, and tells me the waters will bring me healing.

"They love to hear you sing," he tells me. "Sing for your father, your song will reach him in this holy place."

I sing to my father in the flowers, in the waters of the well, knowing that many others have come here to sing, cry, and ask for healing. Offerings of ribbons fly in the wind, along with written messages tied to the trees. Someone asks for prayers for a friend having surgery, another for prayers for a woman giving birth. Tying rags and ribbons to trees at nearby wells is an old tradition, with the belief that as the piece of cloth disintegrates so does the ailment.

Here, by the oldest continuously used holy well in Britain, in constant use for the last 2,000 years, I write my father's name on a white ribbon and tie it to a tree. Perhaps my father's spirit joined the ink in the pen I used to write his name, Derral Wesley Hawkins, and his spirit is now waving in the wind.

I sing to my father's spirit and my song is like the murmuring waters and moaning doves. I am not alone. Birdsong plays above me. A cool breeze, my father's new breath, blows through the trees like an Aeolian harp playing the branches like strings. A grackle drinks from the water. I see my father's face, hear the melody of his life woven into my song, see him drink from the Holy Grail of Chalice Well and know his spirit is alive in the garden of my heart.

Note: This story is an excerpt from the author's forthcoming book, *Sacred Space—Sacred Sound*.

At the Well

CHRISTINE O'BRIEN

The women—barefoot on stone thresholds—
step outside, balance empty clay jars
on their heads, raise tiny dust storms
along edges of trailing hems, move silently
down the hill to the well.

Bodies bend, hands dip into green-gray
water, set brimming pots on stone ledges,
smooth and worn from generations
of mothers, grandmothers. One by one—

Rachel, Ruth, Mary, Magdalena,
Sima, Suhaila—they toss their heads,
let down their veils, dark eyes flashing,
raise eager faces toward the sun,
talk, laugh, embrace.

Moments pass. Finally, with small sighs
and half-smiles, the women pull veils
back into place, reach into shaded
stone recess, lift filled water jugs

to their heads. One by one—
Rachel, Ruth, Mary, Magdalena,
Sima, Suhaila—they turn, drift away
from the old stone well.

Miracle at Lourdes

PAT HARTMAN

It is September 20, 1995, two days before my forty-seventh birthday. I have traveled across an ocean and three countries to be here. Now I look down into a raging river. I wonder if I have made a mistake. My senses are flooded with sights and sounds that shock me. This is not what I expected.

Lourdes, France, is a place of miracle cures. I have worked and waited almost three years to bathe in the holy spring waters of Lourdes. I have envisioned it as holy and inspiring. Looking down from this bridge into the village, it is neither.

When three doctors gave me a hopeless diagnosis and offered to make me as comfortable as possible until the end, I knew God was my only hope. I asked for a plan and found myself going to Lourdes. In 1865, at this very site, Bernadette Soubirous saw the Blessed Virgin Mary. Bernadette had eighteen visions of a white light and a woman dressed in white with a blue sash. I had known about Lourdes and St. Bernadette since I was a child.

I did a little research and found that Lourdes is a town of 1,500 residents, nine hospitals, hotels, shops, and churches. Its only other product besides religious tourist trade is fishing.

Over 5 million pilgrims go to Lourdes each year. The water molecule here is different than most, so the water is absorbed rapidly. There is no need to dry off after you go into the baths.

As I wait for my sister and her husband to get out of the car, I am overwhelmed by the noise and crowds. Shops on the street are selling medals and statues. There is one café with tables on the sidewalk. It sells lunch and ice cream. Medical helpers and volunteers are pushing or pulling gurneys, wheelchairs, and two-wheeled carts. Twisted, paralyzed bodies move along the street with their loved ones who have brought them for a cure, or at least an easing of their pain. I feel morose, shamed by my insignificant little disease that would take me swiftly, compared to the lifetime of suffering these people would endure. Sullen and saddened for all of us here, I look into the raging river.

The water tears at huge boulders. Foam and fog engulf the bridge that takes us to the other side where the grotto is. As Lyn, Bob, and I step onto the bridge, the sound of the river is deafening. The fog is almost a rain as we walk across. We can hardly see each other and have to follow others in front of us to get to the opposite end of the bridge.

There, all is quiet. We step onto the road and everything is hushed. The other people are whispering as if they are in church. There are many people in groups from as small as three to long lines of fifty or more, but all is peaceful. My heart is lightened by this warm, sunny view of people strolling along. Then a gurney goes by: the person is lying down flat, a head poking from a blanket.

This sight takes me back to the desperation that fills this place.

"I have to go to the baths alone," I tell my sister.

Lyn says, "But you can't stand that long, and you can't walk that far. What if you feel tired when you are finished?"

"I will be fine. Go do something, and I'll meet you at the car in two hours."

A row of benches looms ahead, with a sign directing us to line up there until the baths reopened in twenty minutes.

"I came this far. All I have to do is this and then it is done."

"If you can't walk that far, we'll come looking for you. Just sit and wait. If you aren't there at the car, we will find you," Lyn insisted.

"Good. It's always good to have a plan. I will be fine, though."

The line for the baths is filling up fast. A volunteer starts people singing "Immaculate Mary." It is being sung in about five or six different languages. I can see a violet-edged aura around the volunteer. Then I see more and more energies around people's heads and shoulders as they pray a rosary. I am mystified with all that is taking place. Suddenly, we stand and the line moves. There is one side for men and one side for women. Each has several bath areas.

I am pushed into a small area with hooks on the walls and cement benches. The bath is covered with a hospital curtain and six or seven of us are told to disrobe and put on the green hospital gowns that are on the hooks. My purse and clothes are on the bench, but no one here is thinking of stealing anything. The woman next to me has joints that curve backward and wrench around in violent angles.

I am taken into the room with the bath. It is all cement. I step down, turn around, and two volunteers take my arms. They push me backwards, and I trip over a low wall. They catch me by the arms so that all but my nose goes into the water. The water is cold and the fall takes me off guard. Then they ask me to kiss a statue of Mary. Confused, I comply without a second thought.

They pull me out. I remember to look and see if the water dries as fast as I had read it would. I leave one and a half footprints and I am dry. I get dressed and wander out into the world once more.

Out in the sun, I realize I cannot feel my feet or my hands. I have tunnel vision, and my hearing is going off and on. Dazed and traumatized, I decide to sit down before I fall down.

I am in a white thick fog that seems to travel with me. I know the sun is out, but I am shivering and cannot see to walk due to this white shimmering haze that has all but blinded me. I go to the chapel. It is full and people line the walls. Just as I get there, a man gets up and motions me to takes his place. I sit watching the flames on the candles.

I should pray or something wanders through my mind, but I am limp and cannot muster enough energy to pray or even think clearly. I just sit until I feel better.

As I leave the chapel, I can feel energy falling through the top of my head. It is like sparks and electrical rain falling through me. I am energized. I walk stronger and faster. I can see and feel the sun. My pace quickens and I bolt back up the hill. I buy a bottle so that I can take home some of the water to share with others.

I have not felt this strong since I was a teenager. I check the time. It is time to meet Lyn and Bob. I reach the car after almost running across the bridge.

Lyn looks at me. As we pull away, she says, "Oh my God, what happened to you? What happened to you?"

Bob stops her.

"So, Pat, are you hungry? We made dinner reservations at a very nice place."

Bob is squeezing Lyn's hand.

"No, you guys go ahead. I have to go back to my hotel room."

"You haven't eaten in a day and a half. You have to be . . ."

"No, really, there is something I have to do. And we can leave tomorrow."

"What? You said two days?"

"I did what I came to do and now I have to leave."

"Why? What happened?"

"I don't know if you can understand this, but I took it off like a coat and laid it in the waters here at Lourdes, and now I have to let it go."

They do not reply. They buy me some food at a little store and take me back to the hotel. This night is special. I have a date with Mary.

I have a little pink razor with me. I had not been able to shave my legs in over three years because the skin would come off and leave big scars. This is my sign. If I have a miracle cure, there will be no blood.

I run my bath and shave. There is only one tiny red spot. I put the shaver in my purse to remind me, and then I pack to leave in the morning.

That night I see the Blessed Virgin in my dreams, and I feel the energy falling into me. It feels as if I am plugged into a current of energy recharging my battery.

The next morning, I look into the mirror. I see the white energy like a shaft of light reaching from my head up to infinity. I move and it moves with me.

I dress and leave this miracle place of Lourdes, knowing that whatever happens now is not in my hands.

A Spring Thing

DAVID FEELA

The Geyser Springs Trail is a part of the San Juan National Forest, percolating not much more than fifty miles from the hot water faucet that fills my bathtub, yet I had ignored this lofty local wonder for the nearly two decades of life I'd spent in the Four Corners.

Upon learning of this nearby splendor, my imagination filled with visions of Old Faithful. My parents took a much younger me to see that legendary billow of steam, the bubbling cauldron, the wooden walkways creeping across the encrusted stone, to marvel at the magnificent sulfurous shower that spouts off every sixty-seven minutes. Wow, I thought, Colorado has its own geyser!

"Let's go see the geyser before we're too geezerly to appreciate it," I urged my wife one evening.

"Too late," Pam replied, but she agreed to accompany me in case I lost my way back.

We drove early the next morning from Cortez, north on Highway 145, until we reached the West Dolores Road. Pam rode shotgun, guiding me with her modest visitor center brochure. I considered outfitting us with my cache of expedition gear, but then I reconsidered, and we took a simple daypack and some water. Sometimes the natural world needs to be approached on its own terms, without all the high-tech survival clutter that works mostly to keep backcountry equipment manufacturers alive. Besides, the hike was short and the directions appeared rather straight-forward, with the exception of a warning that prompted me to silently question the simplicity of our expedition: "The first part of the trail is on private land and difficult to follow—please do not stray from the path!" Was it dueling banjos I heard in the distance? And where did that image of a shotgun leveled by an old miner with a trickle of chewing tobacco running down his chin come from?

After several failed attempts at finding the trail, we located a promising fence line and followed it. Just as the directions indicated, it wound behind two private cabins, and though we felt a bit like trespassers, we pushed on. Eventually I knew we had hit pay dirt, because, as the trail headed toward the trees, I could hear the rushing water of the Dolores River. The brochure's next warning immediately came to mind: Do not cross during high water.

We stood for a moment and admired the river's meander as it snaked through an open meadow. I've always been drawn to the sound of moving water. Instinctively, I bent to touch it but pulled my hand back, as if shocked by the current.

"Cold?" Pam inquired.

I sent back a clacking Morse code message with my teeth: C . . . O . . . L . . . D, a puff of frosty breath punctuating the spaces between each letter.

Still, we needed to cross. With our boots tied and slung over our shoulders, and our pant legs rolled as high as our calves would allow, we waded into the rushing Dolores. The river quickly kicked at our knees, twisting its glacial muscle against our white, spindly legs. I nearly lost my balance in that first instant of contact, but we steadied each other as best we could and struggled ahead. Our legs ached from the cold, but we managed the distance. On the far bank, we sat down to tie our boots back on, and we laughed like a couple of penguins as we tried to describe how numb our feet felt.

By now the geyser trail seemed obvious enough, worn by quite a few other feet; it started gradually rising as it headed toward the trees. Several seeps along the way made the ground soggy in places, but to accent the dark mud, wildflowers tossed their spring colors like tiny fireworks along the way. The aspens quaked with the slightest breeze, and though we had been laughing, shouting, and chattering, somehow under the shelter of the trees, we both turned silent, as if the canopy forced our thoughts inward.

My thoughts wandered into the trees, those tall sentinels that measure time by quietly adding another ring for every year of life. I believe that trees live inspired lives, their roots tight to the earth, their limbs loose and filtering the air for light. For me, walking in the woods feels like a kind of worship, as if the very idea of cathedrals originated in the human mind when early architects moved among these slender pillars and stared up at the vaulted sky.

But humans more closely resemble geysers. Most of our lives we bubble and spout, then gratefully turn calm—at least that's what I do if there is some pocket of wilderness I can climb into.

Though the trail spanned a mere mile, the internal distance I traversed seemed vast. If I left the earth and came back again, I don't remember. Moving through the dappled patches of sunlight that filtered through the trees must have induced a trance where my feet functioned separately from my mind, as if on autopilot.

I didn't trip over any fallen branches, and I steered

clear of the ruts where early spring rains had washed the ground away. Or rather, I must have levitated over these hazards, because I don't have any clear memory of what difficulties lay along the path; I only noted them on the trip back down the mountain. On the way up I was else-where, circumnavigating the globe, for all I know, caught in deep canyons, listening to waterfalls, stopping in the rainforest where exotic thoughts came to me like so many parrots talking in my head.

Before I realized it, Pam tugged on my sleeve and pointed to an opening in the trees beside a tiny stream. We'd arrived with no one in sight, but we were hardly the first. We saw stones cemented together to shape a reservoir where the water pooled. We approached the edge, where steam rose and mingled with the rank sulfu-rous gases that escaped into the air. A hatch of early flies hovered above the water, interested, no doubt, in what our intentions might be.

"Let's go for a dip," I suggested.

"In that cauldron of scum?"

We stood a while longer, watched the latent broth churn a little as it imitated a lukewarm bowl of split pea soup. Then, as if by a magic spell or a witch's incantation, the water began to boil furiously, and we stared, con-vinced that my suggestion to enter the pool had stirred the gods. I bent once again and touched the water.

"Eighty-two degrees," I speculated.

Whether I had been extraordinarily persuasive or Pam's feet still felt like chunks of ice, I'll never know for sure, but Pam started taking off her clothes. I have never been the kind of man to stand around fully clothed when a beautiful woman is naked, so I stripped down to nothing, and we both stepped carefully into the water.

We found a tolerable perch on a rock below the surface and settled into the soup, up to our necks. The flies swarmed, the sunlight slipped through a crack in the canopy. I pulled two stems of bracken fern from the bank and set one upside-down on each of our heads, a silly party hat to shoo the flies away. We laughed, the geyser splashed, we inhaled the sulfurous steam.

I don't claim Geyser Springs has miraculous restorative powers, but it cured me. What's more remarkable is that I wasn't suffering from anything in particular before I arrived, yet when we left, I somehow felt better. Not healthier, but happier. Not invigorated, but strangely cleansed. I had gone down deep, like an underground seep, and come up with an ounce of wonder—that elixir of spring that consecrates new life.

Nights by Red Sandstone Creek

JUDITH BADER JONES

I flee to Colorado
when daily living feels
taut like wash on a line.
Sleep in a cabin by
Red Sandstone Creek
where water rushes
like a Texas freight train.
Listen to the creek
sing mountain ditties,
echo gold story tales,
water wishes, pebbles
dropped in a well
from universal wanting places.
Heart sounds letting go,
moving past sounds,
easy in shelter
when night settles
like a spare quilt
at the foot of your bed
and water talks you
through the night
like some old friend
passing through,
washing hurts clean.

The Sounds of Goishi

KATE CORBETT

When I moved to Japan, I was searching for something. What that something was, I had no idea, but I thought a new culture and a new set of challenges would surely help me find a way to fill whatever void I was feeling. Fresh out of university, I was out to see the world, quite directionless despite having a job and a vague plan about the future.

In Japan, I lived in a small town right on the coast of the Pacific Ocean. I thought it was novel to be living near the sea, having grown up in a landlocked city with the nearest ocean an eight-hour drive away. I woke up that first morning and I heard the sea gulls crying and smelled the sea. It was fantastic, almost magical.

I had a sudden feeling that things were very right. The house I was living in had no view of the ocean, but I could feel it near. I took a walk that day in the beastly summer humidity of Japan. I found myself meandering to the fishing docks. The cooling breeze off the ocean was refreshing.

I went on for several months not having any significant revelations as to what exactly I was seeking, but all the while I felt as if I were closing in on the answer. After a few months, I decided to buy a car. As an American, I didn't truly feel free until I had an automobile.

One of the first places I took my beat-up Mitsubishi Minica was the seacoast. Although my town was on the ocean, it was a working port with no real public park or beach. I drove to the nearest town and sat on the public beach. I waded out into the harbor with my pant legs rolled up, even when the rest of the beach was deserted. The other beachgoers had long packed in their ocean gear for the season.

I quickly lost feeling in my legs from the frigid temperature. I breathed in the rejuvenating ocean scent. I stayed in the water as long as I could endure the cold, and when the temperature became unbearable, I sat on the sand. I rode the whole way home with the windows up so I could keep the smell of the sea with me as long as possible.

The first few months were lonely, and I found myself using the ocean as a refuge. One day a coworker told me about a stone beach that had an amazing effect on people. It was a little alcove in the mountains about two hours' drive from where we lived. The beach was covered in stones. The stones, churned over and over by the waves, were as smooth as glass. Most of them were jet black, like onyx, and no bigger than a half dollar. All were small enough to fit in the palm of your hand. There were millions of stones packed into the tiny alcove.

When the waves crashed over the rocks and dragged them across each other and the ocean retreated in advance of the next wave, the sound it created was spectacular. I found myself going again and again to this place, the Goishi Coast. I started taking my journal and writing as I listened to the music of the ocean.

Sitting there listening to the rocks moving over each other, sounding like a chorus of a thousand rain sticks being turned over at once, I had my epiphany. I found what I was looking for. Writing. Writing is what I wanted to do. I wanted to make it my living. It had become a part of me. It made me free and allowed me to think deeply and honestly. The rhythm of the water and the sounds of the stones inspired me to artistic heights.

I have long since moved away from Japan, but I have never forgotten my experience at the Goishi Coast. I continue writing to this day, and I make a living doing so. While writing became a part of my soul, so, too, did the ocean. I vowed when I moved from Japan that I would never again live anywhere but at the ocean's side.

I now live within eyesight of the water. I go to the beach almost every day, and I am amazed every day at its power and its ability to renew me and inspire me. I love to lie awake on a hot summer night and hear the waves crashing as the almost constant ocean breeze blows across my bed. I look at the ocean every morning. I am thankful that I went to live by her side and allowed her power to change my life.

Demons from the Sea

MARGO FALLIS

They stood along the shore of the sea, looking much like walking mummies, putrefied and stiff, with rotting black flesh. I grabbed my mother's arm. "Mom, have we come to the land of the living dead?" I asked, unable to take my eyes off the zombies standing before me. My mother laughed and ran toward them.

As I neared the water, I realized my foolish mistake. These were not ethereal beings, demons, or specters: they were people, living and breathing, covered in sticky black mud from the shores of the Dead Sea. Aside from their eyes, bulging from their faces and looking like ping pong balls, no other flesh could be seen.

I glanced at my surroundings. A few people bobbed up and down, like corks in the shallow water, against a backdrop of deep blue sky. A white crust covered the sand, like icing on a cake. Pillars of salt jutted from the water. My mind wandered back to the biblical days of Sodom and Gomorra. Did Lot's wife end up like this—a pillar fixed in the ground?

A row of trickling showers stood near the beach, waiting with patience to wash the mud down their drains. Bougainvillea covered the chain link fences around the limestone brick visitor's center, adding a splash of color. The oppressive heat shrouded the sun-baked land. The rotten-egg smell of sulfur filled my lungs with every hesitant breath. From where I stood, I saw Masada, the Judean Hills, and knew the old city of Jerusalem sprawled on the other side of them.

It was hot, dirty, and smelly, yet everything I saw fascinated me. Here I stood, on the shores of the Dead Sea, the lowest point on earth. I'd spent most of my life living in the mountains, high above sea level, and now I stood 1,320 feet below sea level. I was in Israel, an ancient kingdom filled with history and events beyond my comprehension.

Both my mother and I wanted to spend a day at the Dead Sea. We'd read about it on the Internet. The saltiest sea on earth, it is ten times saltier than the Mediterranean Sea. The Dead Sea contains twenty-one different types of minerals. There are thermomineral springs. No fish or other marine life is sustained in the clear waters.

"Come and join us," someone shouted, bringing me back to reality. I searched for my mother and giggled when I spotted her. She'd rubbed the nigrescent paste over her arms and legs.

I slipped off my sandals and pranced over the burning sands in my swimsuit. Within seconds, my mother and her new friends plastered my body with therapeutic mud. "It'll do you good," Mom said. I stood still, allowing them to enjoy the feel of the muck squishing between their fingers. I looked at my mother, wondering if I looked as ridiculous as she did. I didn't laugh for fear the mud would get in my eyes and mouth. I felt it drying, hardening on my body. My body tingled from the organic elements baking in the desert sun.

"Mom, look at those people," I heard a toddler say. "They look like monsters."

Even though the drying mud cracked and pulled my skin, I laughed. I trotted down to the Dead Sea and looked at my reflection. My pasty hair stuck up in the air like dinosaur spikes. I did indeed look like a monster.

An hour later, I showered and watched the mud swirling in the water around my feet before the drain swallowed it. I went for a dip in the sea and discovered what they'd said was true—I couldn't sink! Floating with my arms and legs spread-eagled, I closed my eyes. I heard goats bleating as they clanked over stones, heading up the hillsides. Birds swooped overheard, cawing in search of a meal. The water lapped onto the beach in gentle rhythms.

This marvelous country, a land filled with a history of battles and wars, and yet hallowed by the world, now held a place in my heart. My own salty tears mingled with the briny sea as I thought of Jesus, the disciples, and others from biblical times. Had they walked along this very beach? I knew in my heart I would never be the same person after that day at the Dead Sea.

Inner Cleansing at Crater Lake

NANCY JACKSON

Water has a voice; it speaks to me, tells stories, sings songs, and soothes my fears. It lifts my spirits and reconnects me to the gods and goddesses of the past and present. Most of all, it brings me into a realm where I am content and at peace with myself. It holds the power to cure, heal, awaken, and revitalize me as nothing else can.

With my partner in tow, I looked forward to my first experience of Crater Lake, a place of mystery, awe, and spectacular beauty. Located in southern Oregon on the crest of the Cascade Mountains, it is full of history and considered a place of spirit power. Native American legend has it that two Chiefs, Llao of the Below World and Skell of the Above World, fought each other in a battle, leading up to the destruction of Llao's home, Mount Mazama. The battle climaxed with the eruption of Mount Mazama and, thus, the creation of Crater Lake.

We had a bounce in our steps as we followed Cleetwood Trail, a somewhat strenuous trek, with the sun warming our skin. As if we were small children waiting for Christmas morning, we couldn't hold back our excitement at seeing the breathtaking gifts left by Mother Nature.

Aware of the area's history as a spirit quest site, I knew we were in for some magic and inner transformations. We were thrust into a bevy of unique and rich colors ranging from aqua, emerald green, sapphire blue, to a deep violet, depending on the direction the sun hit the lake. Chipmunks, tamed by frequent visitors, scampered among the stones and boulders. Each step of the way we were treated to small glimpses beyond the trees, teasers really, capturing bits of the jeweled waters.

Forty-five minutes later, we reached the bottom of the trail, and all I could do was sigh. Tears pooled in my eyes as the realization of what a minute figure I am in such a great, vast world consumed my every emotion.

I perched myself on a rock and let my feet dangle, taking out my journal, feeling compelled to write. My partner busied himself with chiseling more detail in the walking stick we had for the hike back up.

I surveyed the panoramic view, a site that filled me with inspiration, creativity, and strength. Blue skies looked down on us without a cloud to speak of. Birds soared with their wings flared, gliding along on the gentle breeze. I watched one bird touch down and let its feet splash against the water before returning back into the sky. I was envious; I, too, wanted to feel the drops against my skin, to bathe in the sacred water, and envelop myself in the precious liquid of life.

Immersed in the moment, I watched the lake, covered in glitter, with sunrays beating down, dancing upon the ripples and shimmering just for me. The tranquil sound of the water sloshed against the rocks, like a lullaby, bringing me into an inner peace and calm. This was no ordinary place, it was indeed a spirit quest, and I was feeling alive and rejuvenated.

A deep, inner part of me was thanking me, soaking in the goodness, vitality, and recharging from being one with nature. It was in those moments I could escape from all the stresses of my normal daily routine, and just let loose, restore my balance, and appreciate what was set before me.

We stayed there for several hours, not wanting to leave the sanctuary. Somehow, we had lucked out and very few people had taken the trail that day, making it seem as though it were our very own hideaway. I still longed to run and jump in the water, to allow it to wash away all the negativity and slough off the modern person I'd become. Inside, my ancient spirit seemed to beg to be let out and live each day appreciating and admiring the lake forever, to live life in a simple way, without distraction, money, or fear. My spirit could remember a time without electricity, materialism, or food shopping. It sounded like absolute freedom, the kind I was just beginning to taste.

The other part of me wouldn't allow the waters to be tainted. I hadn't done my part yet in this world, and I knew it. The water had purposes far greater than even I could know. Perhaps it held answers to questions I dared not ask.

I made a promise to myself and to the lake. I would return often and search for those answers, invoking the powers that would awaken and stimulate my personal growth. I would strive to uncover the clues and strike a balance, to bring the world my spirit remembered and the only world I've known, together as one.

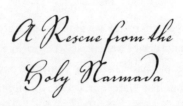

A Rescue from the Holy Narmada

HARISH C. SHARMA

In India, the Narmada is considered one of the holy rivers. Situated on the banks of the holy Narmada is a small village called Mandla. There, following traditional custom, I was married to a woman I had never seen or heard of in my life.

Only a small number of people witnessed the priest chanting mantras from the sacred Vedas to sanctify our marriage. But that was expected, as our wedding occurred on a very warm night in June.

Soon after the midnight wedding, the elders of both families suggested that it would be auspicious if I went to bathe in the holy river Narmada the next day. I saw an opportunity not only to have an early bath, but also to get some relief from the hot, muggy climate.

Being newly wedded, the custom called for me to be accompanied by some immediate members of my family. Many relatives wanted to go along with me. I wanted it to be a little more private and requested that only my youngest brother and two of my sisters accompany me. One of my sisters, Devmani, had just started medical school.

After breakfast early the next morning, we went to the spot in the river that my father-in-law had suggested. He had told us it was one of the safest and least crowded places on the holy river. True to what I had been told, no one else showed up in that area.

As can be expected during the warm days of June, the level of water in the river was low, and the flow was moderate. My two sisters and I were not good swimmers, so we swam close to the shore. My brother, who was a good swimmer, ventured farther out.

Diving into water on a day when the thermometer is over 100 degrees is in itself a delight, and we were enjoying every bit of it. Now and then, my brother would come and check on us, just to make sure that we were safe, even though we were in the shallow region of water. After all, I was the newly married person.

Suddenly, we heard cries of help but did not know where it came from. As we turned our heads, we noticed that my brother was waving his hands feverishly and shouting. Knowing that he was such a good swimmer, we were sure nothing would happen to him in such a moderate flowing river. When we heard his shouts, we thought that he was crying wolf.

Though he was going beneath the surface of the water, we still thought that he was just kidding. We thought that nothing could happen. After all, he was a strong, young seventeen-year-old kid. Soon he completely disappeared, and we could not even hear him. Devmani said that maybe he was drowning. But we could not find out, as none of us knew how to swim to that spot and check on him, and there was no one in sight on our side of the river.

We came out of the river and noticed that there was a young man standing on the other side. We shouted to him and pointed to my brother. That young man immediately jumped into the river and swam to the spot where my brother was. The stranger pulled him out and brought him ashore on our side of the river. After laying my brother on the sand, he left.

Devmani had heard about CPR, but none of us knew how to do it. When she saw my brother's blue face, she immediately asked me and our other sister, Rajbala, to assist her in getting my brother to stand on his head. The three of us somehow managed to get him on his head. Then Devmani told us to pound on my brother's chest as hard as we could. His mouth was closed tight. With all my might, I opened his mouth and started pounding on his chest. We were crying and holding my brother straight up on his head and pounding on his chest and trying to keep his mouth open, all at the same time.

We must have been trying all this for at least five minutes when we saw an enormous amount of water and food coming out of my brother's mouth. We stopped pounding on his chest, and my brother's body fell to the ground. We turned his face upwards, and Devmani started breathing into his mouth, asking me to keep pounding on his chest.

Just then, we saw a couple of kids come running. In such a small town, they knew that I had been married the previous night. We asked them to rush to my in-laws' place and get medical help.

Soon, one of my brothers-in-law, who was a doctor, arrived. By that time, my brother had started to breathe on his own, but was still unconscious. Someone brought a stretcher, and my brother was taken to the nearby hospital.

There was a much bigger crowd to visit my brother in his hospital bed. All were of the opinion that my brother had survived because of my wife. We found out that prior to our marriage, she had prayed at the banks of the holy Narmada.

If my brother had not survived that day, my wife would have been blamed for that mishap. She would have been branded a woman of misfortune and would have had to live with that scar all her life. The holy Narmada saved her, as her prayers had saved my brother and given me an unforgettable first day of marriage.

Fountain of the Enclosed Valley

SARA TAVI

It was too early to go back to the hotel and swim. The day was hot, in the nineties, and we had already been to the scenic Abbaye de la Senanque, a monastery tucked into the mountains. The Cistercian monks were famous for growing and harvesting lavender, and their spare sanctuary had remained almost the same since the eleventh century.

We had come to this beautiful land for a family vacation: Peter, our three children, and I. We spent day after day exploring the countryside, its colors an explosion of bold blues, yellows, and oranges.

Our first day was abnormally hot for the area. Luckily, the ice cream vendor in the nearby town of Rousillon was ready for us. Our berry sorbet cones matched the ochre hills, soothed our hot throats, and cooled us from the inside out.

The next day was cooler, and I could finally feel the romance of Provence. The temperature of heaven. No humidity, slight breeze, seventy-eight degrees. We leaned into canvas chairs on the patio, eating cherries, drinking white wine. Almond trees and rosemary surrounded us. Valley and mountains made this a serene perch, millennium of calm civilization. Tall grasses and bamboo marked the edge of the garden.

Back in the car, we drove to Fontaine De Vaucluse (Fountain of the Enclosed Valley), a town with a river running through it, a lush haven in an arid hillside. As we walked from the parking lot outside the town, we crossed the river and started climbing toward the source, and Peter told us the mysterious story. The resurgent spring that emerged from the rocks up ahead came from so deep within the earth that no one knew how deep the water reached. Divers had gone down 200 meters and had to return because they ran out of oxygen. While they were ascending, they experienced symptoms of the bends (pressure illness).

The spring was the source of the River Sorgue. Peter pointed out a huge obelisk built to honor the medieval poet Petrarch, who had lived here for sixteen years, from the age of thirty-three, while he longed for his pious muse, Laura. She died of the plague in Avignon in 1348, their relationship never consummated, as she was married to someone else.

We looked down into clear, clean water flowing beneath our feet. As we approached the edge of the fifteen-foot-wide bowl, I slipped on the wet rocks and warned the others. This wishing well would snatch us if we were not careful.

Still, there was something ancient and magical and surreal about this place, waters from the deep rising and spilling down through the town, cheap souvenirs and pleasant cafés sparkling at the edges. Peter didn't tell me until later that he and the kids had crept to the very edge of the water's source, knowing I would have worried about them drowning.

Instead, I enjoyed the peaceful moment alone, gazing up at the mountains, realizing that I was more relaxed than I had been for weeks, maybe months. Planning the trip, finishing my work at home, and helping the kids to finish at their schools had gone smoothly but had gotten me wound up tight.

A stanza of a new blues song I had written came back to me: "I'm tight as a rubber band, pulled back and ready to spring, Yes I'm tight as a rubber band, pulled back and ready to spring, But where am I going and what do I need to bring?" Nothing, I need to bring nothing, I answered silently, looking down into the deep water. I needed to open to the waters all around me, from that underground spring, the fountain gushing up through the rocks, the river running down through the town. I felt my own internal waters rise up around the rocks of tension that I called my body. As I rejoined my family, I felt lighter, more fluid. I even laughed, instead of complaining, over the payment required to use the public bathroom over-looking the river.

As we drove through the mountains, back to the town of Gordes and our hotel, I thought about Petrarch and Laura, his muse. I was taking a vacation from my modern muse, my therapist. She had inspired me to lis-ten to my own tentative, childlike creative voice, to write songs and paint pictures, and to listen to the messages my body and dreams contained. It was slow, deep work, unearthing hidden treasures and painful memories. My love for her and trust in our powers to unravel together all that was available but blocked within my middle-aged person had carried me far. Far away from her and from my work to this oasis in Provence. My muse, like Laura, was married to someone else, but inspired me anyway. Perhaps Petrarch had wandered along the river's edge as I had, soaking up the rich fountain's wet energy like a sponge, filling the space created by Laura's absence with poetry, meaning, cleansing.

Often, during vacations away from my therapist, I had panicked, sure that my chances for joy and relief from my neurotic past had vanished. Intellectually, I knew we would soon resume our work together, but emotionally I would become bereft, wondering if one of us would die before the vacation would end. Being married to a warm, generous partner was little comfort at those moments.

This vacation, though, I had not despaired. Something was shifting, different. I was actually getting healthier. The work of hours, weeks, and years had managed to change me, to make me feel more whole, a solid endurable changing self, even when I was on vacation.

Back at the hotel, the kids settled into bed, tired from exploring and dinner. Peter sneaked into their room with his camera to take a picture, three kids in three twin beds, lined up next to each other. Rachel and James with sheets over them, heads poking out, mouths open, like porpoises coming up for air, white sheets the waves they floated on. Rachel's hands were crossed at the wrists, fingers touching each other, ready to dive into dreamland. Don, tanned and dressed in flannel pajama pants and a big T-shirt, was slightly curled on top of the sheets, hair longer than it had ever been.

Later that night I woke, seeing images and colors dance through my head so fast I watched quietly, like I'd crept in to see a movie I wasn't supposed to see. Not asleep, yet sure that I had never been awake in this way before, I watched my cravings and marveled at how ancient and alive they appeared, wanting fountains to engulf me, to support me as I rose and opened.

Energy was suddenly flowing into and out of and all around me, and time disappeared. Was I now the fountain of the enclosed valley? Was Peter? Where did this river of energy begin and end? What was the source? Had I carried the sensational memory of the Fontaine de Vaucluse in my body, releasing it into the room as I changed into my nightgown? Perhaps the room itself was transformed by the stream of moonlight that filtered through blue curtains, magically enlivening our quiet evening.

The light shone onto Peter's bare shoulder, inviting me to touch his suntanned skin. Now that I was a whole person, waters flowing, inside and out, I could invite Peter to share in the celebration. He, too, was energized, joining me as if we were two streams running out of the same source, waters flowing between us, all around us, in the forms we created together. Coupled, we rode the rapids, swept over boulders, and sent drops of sparkling water out into the night.

Behold the Living Waters

DEBORAH SHOUSE

When my friend Brian hears I am going to visit a *mik-vah*, the sacred cleansing bath that Jewish women use to purify themselves after their menstruation period, he is outraged.

"I thought you were a feminist," he says accusingly. He has the same look of sturdy determination that I see in the peasant face of my great-grandfather in his one surviving photo.

"The idea of a woman's menstrual blood being unclean," Brian paces, waving his arms like a rabbi punctuating a sermon, "the idea of the Bible controlling the sexual relationships between men and women—that seems archaic and antifeminist to me."

I hear the passion in his voice—I too have felt that way. But, though I don't believe menstruating women are unclean, though *mikvah* never came up in my own Reform upbringing, I feel a longing to understand the ancient ritual. I hold an image of my great-grandmother in her poor Russian village, bundled against the bitter cold, pushing her way through the wind to get to the small building that housed the *mikvah*. Was the water warm enough that she could keep God and prayers in her mind, or did it prickle her skin into goosebumps?

I have read about *mikvahs* in Isaac Singer books and pictured a dark room, with a pool of water resting in rough stone. The stone is tinged green with minerals, and the steps leading down into the pool are worn from the bare feet of hundreds of women. I imagine a long line of Jewish ancestors, immersing and rededicating themselves to God. I want to see where that ceremony might have taken place.

I meet Anna, the wife of the Hasidic rabbi in our community, at the low gray building behind their synagogue. She ushers me into a pleasant anteroom that looks like the entrance to a low-key spa.

"So you want to see the living waters?" Anna says. "That's one way to call the *mikvah* waters."

The phrase sounds like an advertisement for a theme park: the living waters. I smile, envisioning Jewish women whisking down long slides, frolicking through tall plumes of water, bouncing up and down in the artificial surf.

"Yes," I say, and she beckons me to sit on the sofa. She sits across from me and leans forward, her hands clasped in her lap, her voice earnest.

"Water is considered the embodiment of kindness. The *mikvah* is at the core of the Jewish community," she says. "It's one of the three *mitzvots*, divine commands, allocated especially for the woman. The others are the lighting of the holiday candles and the baking of the *challah*. But the *mikvah* is special, because it's the only mitzvot that involves the entire body, total immersion."

I feel a sense of comfort when I hear that phrase: total immersion.

Three mornings a week, I go to the health club pool. I start by sitting on the edge, one leg testing the water temperature, while I wonder if I really want to get cold and wet. When I plunge in, my swimming is an act of discipline rather than a rite of spirituality.

"Can I see the actual *mikvah* now?" I ask, wanting to be near this water.

She nods, unlocks a door, leads me down a short hallway where I am surprised to see an ordinary-looking bathroom. Ordinary except for the *mezuzah* on the doorpost and the list of *mikvah* rules posted beside the sink.

"Before going to the *mikvah*, the woman comes here and washes herself thoroughly," Anna says. I read the list, noting that the woman may not enter the *mikvah* until the night is dark and the stars are out. The list says she must wash all the crevices of her body, including between her fingers and toes, behind her ears, and the other crevices that modesty prevents describing. She must comb the hair on all parts of her body. After she is thoroughly cleaned, she takes a shower.

After the shower, Anna tells me, an attendant checks her, looking carefully at her back and arms and legs, to make sure no fallen hair, no little flake of dry skin gets in the way of her skin and the water having their complete connection.

I hold this idea—nothing comes between the woman and the water, nothing comes between the woman and God. I think of a lover I haven't seen in a month: the hungry ache to get close and closer, how every inch of skin must meet, must connect, that feeling of relief at no longer being alone.

I hold my breath as Anna leads me into the *mikvah* room. But just as quickly, I have to bite my tongue to keep from saying, "This is not how it's supposed to look!" This pool looks so ordinary, so unmystical, so like the hot tub that I can clamber into any morning after I work out.

The *mikvah* has none of the poetry or character that I had so long imagined. It's all polite, clean tile instead of history-steeped stone. Once the tub is initially filled with rainwater, they add other water, plus the necessary chemicals to keep it sanitary.

"Is the *mikvah* a spiritual experience for you?" I ask Anna, wondering if she knows there are so many other places she could immerse herself in hot water.

"Yes," she says. She closes her eyes and her voice grows soft. "I feel pure, clean, and uplifted after I immerse myself. The immersion is an act of faith and purification. Afterwards, I cover my head with a wash-cloth and say a prayer. The whole ceremony is one of the only times I'm alone, in silence, with my own thoughts and prayers."

As she speaks, I think of my only ritual immersion, which took place in a hot springs near the Rio Grande River.

My lover and I were in Taos and heard about this natural hot springs. Our last afternoon in town, we set out. Our directions were cryptic: turn right at the buffalo skull on the ground next to the wooden mailbox before you get to the fourth gravel road, then go past the fourth adobe and turn left at the boulder shaped like a crow.

As city people, we each had different ideas of what a gravel road was and what the shape of a crow meant—so it was dark before we finally reached the dirt road that wound us close to the river.

The moon illuminated the narrow path that wiggled through the rocks, coaxing us toward the water. Three bearded men passed us, towels flung over their bare shoulders, and gave us the final directions. The small pool was almost hidden in the rocks, and we could hear the rushing of the river just a few feet below. It felt strange to be undressing outdoors, and I slipped hurriedly into the water.

Then I felt the water embrace me. That embrace held me in the light of moon and stars, only the hurrying river breaking the exquisite stillness.

"Let's baptize ourselves," he suggested. We each chose something we wanted to leave under the water and something we wanted to bring out of the water.

We held hands and took turns immersing each other. I left shame on the bottom of that pool and emerged with grace and laughter. I stood up into the moonlight, imbued with a new sense of courage and openness that shone through me as the moon shone on me. That immersion marked me and allowed me to see that water and ritual could change me.

But once we left the springs, I never thought of bringing a water ritual into my everyday life of bathtubs and swimming pools.

Now, I kneel and stick my hand in the *mikvah* water, imagining it is pure, collected from a thousand rainfalls. This is the water women come into, after their period and before they return to their husband's bed. In biblical days, in the desert, it would have taken a long time to collect such water. To be immersed in water then would have seemed more extraordinary, more holy.

"*Mikvah* creates the rhythm of the marriage relationship," Anna says. "The young couples sometimes have a hard time with it, but after a while, you come to see it as nice. It makes you look forward to getting together." I imagine women of centuries ago coming in the night to immerse themselves in the holy water, and then, once they are clean, returning to their husbands for lovemaking for the first time in days.

As we leave, Anna turns, kisses her hand, and presses it on the *mezuzah*.

The next day, I decide to try an immersion ritual in the swimming pool. The early morning energy of the pool is frenetic. Lean men in small suits claim the lap lanes, churning through the water like speedboats. In another area of the pool, people in a water aerobics class move their arms and bounce their feet in time to a Supremes song, which I can hear even underwater. There is no air of calm and quiet, no sense of spiritual possibilities here. Still, this is the deepest body of water I will be in during my immersion rituals. After my swim, I take off my goggles and swim cap and stand in my lane. I imagine I am alone and naked, properly scrubbed and combed, with nothing between me and the water. Then I go under. I squat on the bottom of the pool, sculling so I don't pop up to the surface, and imagine I am a pious Jewish woman, coming clean. I rise to the surface, envisioning myself a purer, more insightful person.

My eyes are still closed when I hear a voice say, "Excuse me, excuse me." I open my eyes and see a man holding a kick board. "Are you done with this lane?" He pulls on his goggles and poises on the edge.

"Yes," I say, "I am done."

So I give up on the swimming pool. The next evening I try my ritual at home. My bathtub does not have the full amount of natural water prescribed by the Torah. I can't stand before God and immerse myself in this tub; but I can lie down and go under the water.

I light a candle and fill the tub with more water than I am used to. I turn out the ceiling light. The candle creates an odd shadow on the wall, like a beard flapping in wind.

I sink into the tub, carefully, so no liquid spills.

I sit for a while, with a feeling of calm pleasure. Then I lean back, hold my nose, and go under. I hear the quiet splash of water seeping over the rim, I feel cradled in the cocoon of warmth. Skin to water, that is the *mitsvot*, the connection I am seeking. Let nothing come between this powerful and holy connection, I pray.

For those few moments, nothing does.

A Sacred Bond

TAMMY MURRAY

Patty and I have been friends for years. Although we are at different places in our lives, Patty with little ones and me with grown children, we have much in common. We appreciate our friendship because of our differences as well as our similarities. I love to hear the stories that she shares about the funny things her little guys say and do. I know she appreciates my experience as a mother of successful adult children.

We work at the same retirement community and have bonded over many projects we have tackled together, and even over an occasional disagreement. No level of bonding, however, can take the place of the unity we have found in our shared worship of "tubby time."

We had been friends for several years before either of us felt secure enough to let the other in on our secret. It happened gradually, of course. You don't just blurt something like this out all at once. Different in so many ways, we never dreamed that we quietly harbored the same passion.

Bubbles and bath salts were the stuff of our private lives. Our husbands knew. Our children knew. But friends were not privy to knowledge about this delightful pastime. When we finally revealed ourselves, each to the other, there was much jubilation at finding a kindred spirit.

When my first child came along, my world got pretty busy. Like all mothers, my life was filled with laundry and bottles and burping and walking the floors late at night. There was no time for me anymore. My survival instincts drove me to the water.

There in my bath, undisturbed, I could soak myself in mountains of bubbles, read a juicy magazine article, or just close my eyes and escape to magical places where people slept through the night and ate meals sitting at a table with lit candles. In this imaginary world, people never had to grab a forkful as they paced past their plate, bouncing a fussy baby on their hip.

The years passed quickly. Life is much different for me now. I go to sleep when I choose and wake when my alarm goes off, no babies crying for a midnight snuggle. My husband and I have lovely dinners, just the two of us, and find ourselves lonely for the company of our children. We look forward to college vacations when the house will be full and messy again.

These days I have time to take some classes at our local community college. I'm learning to play the piano and have taken up crocheting again.

Patty envies me for my peaceful world, and my heart longs for a bit of her busyness. The boys and her part-time job keep her fully occupied. Playdates, doctors' appointments, and potty training fill her days to overflowing, until she dreams of being back at work. Phone messages from the sitter bring immediate panic. She returns the call to hear news that one has a fever and the other is in time-out. At these moments, she longs for nothing more than to quit her job, scoop them up and hustle them home, never to abandon them again.

In the early evening, however, our spirits merge as we abandon our cares and woes, and return to the shrine where we worship. The chrome faucet, fluffy towels, a scented candle, and a glass of wine are the elements that furnish our tiled chapel. We kneel and stir the water. The bath salts dissolve, the mirror steams up, and we are apart from the world again. We reconnect with ourselves, relax, think, ponder, and eventually we rejoice. Baptism is complete and our souls are inspired and refreshed. Our escape to the quiet solitude of the water has reminded us, once again, of the wonderful lives we will return to shortly.

After dinner the phone rings. I know it will be Patty, and the call will begin predictably, "Have you taken your tubby yet?"

"Did you read tonight?"

"I think I might light my new candle."

It feels good to have a friend who seeks renewal in the same way I do. We all need to know that we are not alone as we walk through life. Finding a soul mate, as I have in Patty, brings a comforting sense of companionship, a sense that "there's someone out there who gets me."

Recently I have discovered that there may be another spirit who shares this special ritual of mine. My college-aged daughter has been dipping into my bath oils and monopolizing my tub whenever she's home for a visit. The hectic pace of college life has apparently driven her to the water. She has recognized that there are times when there is nothing better than to return to the womb, to retreat, to immerse herself in warmth and solitude.

My heart exults in knowing that she has learned this lesson from years of observing me turn briefly away from my responsibilities and disappear behind the bathroom door. As she goes forward in her life, becoming a busy doctor, mom, or whatever she chooses to be, I will take quiet joy in knowing that there is a special someone out there who understands me and that I understand her. I will celebrate knowing that I have passed this important part of who I am to my child, and that she has received it with an open heart and a soft, fluffy towel.

Meditation:

TAKING A RITUAL BATH

Most of us have given ourselves the luxurious treat of taking a relaxing, meditative bath, but how many of us have seen it as a sacred water site?

Here are some ideas for ritual bathing, collected from my own thoughts and from author and herbalist Stephanie Rose Hunt Bird.

- ~ Put a sacred symbol—a rosary, prayer beads, Tibetan bowl, or other symbol of your choosing— in or near the bathwater.

- ~ Put some river rocks in the bath with you, or collect a few in a bowl of water and place near the tub where you can see them. For a healing bath, place crystals or other gemstones with specific healing properties in the bathwater.

- ~ Even if you're far from the ocean, a container of seashells collected from your favorite beach, or a glass bowl of beach sand, can be a visual reminder of the ocean's timeless beauty or the peace you felt on your last vacation.

- ~ Add your favorite music, whether it's classical flutes or Caribbean steel drums. Or place Tibetan bells, chimes, or a rainstick near the tub, and enjoy their "live" sound as you bathe.

- Add lavender or your favorite essential oil. Experiment to find oils that leave you soothed and comforted, or stimulated and refreshed. Your local supplier will have suggestions to guide you.

- Light candles or, for a refreshing change, extinguish all the lights and sit in the dark. Cup your hands in the water, and listen to the sound of it trickling back into the tub.

African Water Orisha

Stephanie Rose Hunt Bird

As I ponder the power and mystery of water, a trip near my ancestral home seems in order. First, there is Yemoya/Olokun, the black mermaid who is also considered the Great Mother. Then there is another peculiar fellow lurking about the water. Not quite male or female, Erinlé is the great hunter *orisha* (god). This hermaphrodite reigns above ground and in the water—a most unusual ability. On land, Erinlé resides in the forest and on farms. In the sea, Erinlé lives with Yemoja/Olokun. The androgynous deity Erinlé, honored as the orisha of herbalism and custodian to animals, she is also linked to the fertility of humans and responsible for the abundance of life in oceans and rivers.

With Yemoja/Olokun and Erinlé in mind, I developed a Water Orisha Wash that can be used as a full body wash. This sweet water combines sea kelp and Irish moss—two gifts of Yemoja/Olokun—with wholesome nutrients from Erinlé, perfumed with the green scent of the banks of yet another water *orisha*, the river goddess of love, Oshun.

ORISHA SWEET WATER WASH

~

1 cup distilled water
1/2 cup soapwort root
1/2 cup Irish moss (powdered)
1/4 cup coconut milk
1 tablespoon strained lemon or lime juice
1/4 cup orange blossom water
1/4 cup powdered sea kelp

SCENT
Makes approximately 10 ounces; shelf life: 1 month
kept cool
6 drops ocean scented perfume or ocean fragrance
oil *or* 2 drops each juniper, boise de rose, vetiver,
ocean pine essential oil

1. Boil water. Add soapwort root; reduce heat to low.
   Brew thirty minutes. Turn off heat; steep an addi-
   tional fifteen minutes.
2. Strain soapwort through a sieve. Return infusion
   to pot; boil.
3. Add Irish moss one tablespoon at a time, stirring
   vigorously with each addition. Reduce heat to
   low; cover; allow to thicken for thirty minutes.
4. Use a mixer or beat by hand in a separate bowl: coconut milk, fruit juice, and orange blossom water. Add to
   strained soapwort mixture. Add sea kelp a tablespoon
   at a time. Blend until smooth. Add perfume.
5. Let mixture sit while you prepare for your
   bathing ritual.

RITUAL BATH WITH ORISHA WASH

To prepare the bathtub, wet the surface with a sea sponge. Sprinkle sea salt in and around the tub. Scrub the tub and surrounding area until it is clean. Rinse the tub and spritz the bath area with rosewater, diluted flower essences, holy water, or rainwater. Run a steaming hot bath, climb in, and lie back. Take deep cleansing breaths. Close your eyes and focus on clearing your mind as you soak in the power of your sacred water space.

For deep cleansing, begin with the crown of your head. What do you want lifted from you? What would make you feel lighter, clearer, or more at ease? Make a plea for your desire, three times. Finish by saying blessed be, or thank you.

Wet your hair and pour on the Orisha Sweet Water Wash. Visualize your troubles being washed away as you rinse the suds from your hair. As the bubbles trail down your body, let your worries and anxieties slide into the waters beneath you. Grab a natural sponge and lather up. This is your time to be quiet and still within yourself; allow the spirits to move you. When you are done, pull the plug and visualize your troubles draining out with the water.

Part Four

THE MYSTERY OF WATER: STORIES OF MAGIC AND MYSTERY

Sacred Water, Sacred Feet

MARIL CRABTREE

We walk single file under the summer sun, twelve men and women who have chosen to memorialize the dropping of the world's first atomic bombs on Hiroshima and Nagasaki by "walking for peace" from August 6 to August 9.

Yesterday, it was bearable. The temperature was in the low nineties, and a cloud cover appeared in the hottest part of the day. With straw hats, good shoes, and plenty of sunscreen, we found that we could walk eighteen miles that day.

But this morning, the aches and pains of walking that far have made a new home in our bodies. The blisters that threatened to appear the first day come on full force the second day. Temperatures soar while the sun blazes in a cloudless sky.

We walk more slowly now, hoping to cover at least sixteen miles, but aware that hot sun on melting asphalt is taking its toll. Every mile or so, Margaret, our faithful "sag wagon" lady, meets us in her van and ladles out cold water to keep us going. After we drink our fill, we splash ourselves and soak our bandannas in it. Still, the heat bores down from above and shimmers up from below, trapping us like lobsters in a boiling pot.

By late afternoon, the temperature reaches an impossible 105 degrees. Two among our small group have succumbed to heat exhaustion and now ride with the sag wagon. The rest of us trudge on, determined to make it to the designated stopping point.

Finally, at the end of a long hill that felt more mountainous with each step, we stumble into the vans that take us to the church basement where we'll sleep that night. The brief ride to the church is mostly filled with moans of "Oh, my aching feet!" in a dozen variations.

As we climb down from the vans and assemble in front of the basement door, Margaret pauses and grins.

"We have something special for you peace pilgrims," she says.

Flinging the door back, she leads us into the large, cool basement space. There, arranged in a circle, are twelve folding chairs. In front of each chair sits a white enamel washbasin filled with cool water.

A hush precedes us as we file into the room. Slowly, with a few groans, we lower our bodies into the chairs and take off shoes and socks. For a few moments, the only sound is "Ahhhhh" as we plop our sore, hot, tired feet into that water.

The blessings have only begun. Armed with bars of soap and soft towels, Margaret and her helpers give each of us a gentle but thorough foot washing. They tenderly wash the blisters and calluses on each foot, then dry them and dust them with talcum powder.

This ancient ritual of foot washing, given as a practical sign of hospitality to travelers of dusty Middle Eastern roads, has never been so welcome.

Too tired to say much, all we can do is say thank you over and over for this gift of sacred water and the hands that prepared it for us. I, who thought of myself as a servant of peace, now know who the real servants are: those who made it possible for us to keep putting one foot in front of the other.

Initiation

MIKI ONIANYA CONN

Seven years ago, I was initiated into the Yoruba priest-hood, as a priestess of Oshun. Oshun is the African god-dess of fertility, prosperity, and sensuality. She is also the river goddess—the goddess of all fresh waters, the waters of life.

Her symbols include the pumpkin or calabash, which represents the womb, and her substance is honey, bringing sweetness, abundance, prosperity, and sensuality. Her colors are orange, gold, coral (the colors of the sunrise and sunset), and green (the color of new growth, fertility, and prosperity). Her number is five, and she is related to Venus. She laughs like sparkling water, and her tears often flow for her people.

In the Yoruba tradition, I am a daughter of Oshun, which means that she plays a major part in my daily life and in my very essence. My personality, moods, and experiences reflect her role in my life.

We become initiated for a variety of reasons, one being to acknowledge the importance of Spirit in our lives, to consciously work with Spirit in our own growth, and to assist others in their life path. My experiences before and after my initiation demonstrate the power of Oshun, river goddess, in my life and confirm that I am indeed one of her daughters.

Two years before my initiation, while assisting in a

women's spiritual retreat in Hawaii, we went to a lake to honor Laka, the Hawaiian goddess who bears many similarities to Oshun, as well as Oshun herself. We brought offerings of fresh fruits to place on banana leaves. The lake was sheltered in a rocky and wooded cove. A waterfall tumbled into the lake at one end, and lake water trickled away in a rocky stream at the other end—truly the house of Oshun/Laka. Several large stones protruded from the lake, and although the day was gloriously sunny, the water was icy cold.

Omifunke, priestess of Yemaya, soon to be my godmother, had organized this retreat with me. She directed me to carry the offerings out to one of the large stones in the middle of the lake. I demurred. First of all, I can't swim and the water was clearly over my head. Secondly, I suffer from Raynaud's syndrome, which renders my extremities numb in cold water. Even if I *could* swim, I would not have the use of my hands and feet long enough to carry out the task.

She insisted firmly, saying, "Don't you trust Oshun? She will take care of you."

With a deep breath of resignation, I stepped into the water. I discovered steppingstones that led me safely to the largest of the stones, on which I found the word "Laka" inscribed. The water was over my shoulders, but by bracing myself against the large stone, I was able to manage. I became totally focused on the task at hand— placing each woman's offering on the stone, as, one by one, they entered the lake and came to me.

What drama! The women were squealing with the cold of the water, shivering uncontrollably, teeth chattering. Suddenly I realized that I, the one with Raynaud's, who is excessively sensitive to cold, was quite comfortable.

The others marveled at how relaxed I was in the water, since their only desire was to get out as quickly as possible and warm up in the sun on the shore.

When all of the offerings had been placed, I was free to leave the water, but by now I was so comfortable and at peace that I had no desire to get out. My godmother smiled at me, and said, "See, trust in her and Oshun will take care of you."

In my third year as a priestess, my new lover, struggling to understand what it meant to be in relationship with a priestess, told me that a couple he was friends with, was pregnant for the seventh time. Each pregnancy had ended in miscarriage, and he and his friends were afraid to even hope that this pregnancy could be successful. He asked if there was anything in my religion that could help.

I told him he had come to the right place. Oshun governs conception and childbirth, and as a priestess of Oshun, I might, indeed, be able to help. Since I didn't know the couple and they had not come to me, and since they might be suspicious of my spiritual tradition, I felt an indirect approach was necessary. I told him that while it would be unethical to perform rituals without their consent, we could go to the river with offerings and ask Oshun to intercede. I knew that prayer was often powerful enough to make a difference.

We went to the Mohawk River, near my home, bringing five oranges (symbolic of Oshun) and honey. I poured the honey over the oranges and floated them in the river, praying to Oshun and speaking in plain English of my desire for a good outcome in this pregnancy. Then I asked my friend to speak on their behalf, since they were his friends. He did so, awkwardly at first and then with increasing conviction. When we finished, we looked out across the river where the sun sparkled on the little waves like diamonds. It was breathtaking. "Do you believe in omens?" he asked.

The pregnancy went well, and in due time, a beautiful baby girl was born, followed a year and a half later by a second child.

That experience and others have brought me closer to Oshun and increased my reverence for the mysterious forces that affect our lives. With each experience, my understanding of the purpose of the water goddess deepens, as does my commitment to live my life in partnership with her. She is within me and I am a part of her.

I used to fear water, avoiding it and seldom even drinking it. Now, thanks to Oshun, I value fresh water as the substance that makes life possible, as an expression of our emotions, as our first earthly home in the uterus, as the link and common thread to all life. I smile and lift my face when the rain falls and accept it as a sign that Oshun is here.

May the blessing of clean water continue to flow in small and large ways, cleansing, healing, lubricating, supporting, and moving us on. *Maferefun Oshun!* Praise and thanks to Oshun.

A Fish Named Buddy

Dawn Allcot

His name was Buddy. I won him at a carnival by throwing a Ping-Pong ball into a little goldfish bowl. By the time I got home from the fair, the pet store was closed, so Buddy spent the night in a juice glass until I could buy him a tank in the morning.

Twelve hours and $50 later, Buddy had a ten-gallon home kept clean by two high-powered filters, decorated with blue rocks, and populated by a tiny plastic mermaid and three golden friends.

My financial luck started the next day. I found $10 in an old pair of jeans and another five in a coat I hadn't worn since the previous spring. The big money came when I sat down the following night to do my taxes.

I plugged the digits from my W-2 onto the 1040-EZ short form, and did the math by hand on an old envelope. I stared at the four digits. A giddy feeling traveled up my body. *That can't be right.* In the past, I'd received refunds as high as $300, and had been happy with the "found money." My heart pounded with excitement at the possibility of the amount on the page. I rechecked my math with a calculator.

"TJ!" I called out to my husband. "I'm getting $1,200 back on my taxes! Twelve hundred dollars! Can you believe that?"

"Cool," he replied. "That'll help things."

The next day, I told my friend Erica about my good fortune.

"Where did you say you put the fish tank?" she asked.

"In the back corner of the living room."

"To the right or left of your front door?"

"Um, right."

"Oh, that explains it. That's the southeast corner of your living room. Water in the southeast corner enhances wealth, according to the principles of feng shui."

"OK," I said, skeptical.

Although the other fish in the tank died quickly, Buddy prospered. Friends often commented on our carnival goldfish that had reached the size of a baby Koi.

As he grew, so did our wealth. Raise followed raise at work, for both of us. I received two promotions in a few months. Freelance opportunities appeared—my husband fixed a few computers on the side, while I fell into freelance writing jobs. Money poured in like a waterfall. We didn't exactly hit the lottery, but it was enough to keep us well fed, well traveled, and out of debt for two years.

One morning, I awoke to discover that Buddy didn't look so well. His bright scales had turned sickly pale, the shade of an under-ripe orange. Rather than darting from side to side in the tank, he hovered inches from the top of the water line. His gills opened wide then slammed shut, as if every breath were a struggle.

By evening, he was flopping in the water, tilting and turning. As his breath and movement grew more sporadic, I stared at him and prayed, "Please, God, just let the poor fish die. Let his suffering be over."

"He's just a fish," my husband reminded me.

"I know," I said, wiping a tear from my eye. "But he was Buddy. He's part of the family, and he's been here so long."

The change was subtle. First, one of my editors changed jobs—going to work for a company that didn't hire freelancers—and another simply stopped calling me with assignments. After the dot-com boom, the publishing industry hit hard times. I foresaw the demise of the magazine I edited, and got out on my own terms.

Burned out and disheartened, I took a low-paying job in a retail store and began marketing myself furiously as a freelance writer. But running a start-up business from our living room wasn't easy, and many magazines simply didn't have the budget for another freelancer.

With TJ's steady job, we scraped by, but I hated not having my "own" money in my pocket and not being able to contribute 50 percent to household expenses.

Then the drought spread to both of us. Expenses, both planned and unplanned, grew. Car repairs, a new truck, and a flood in the apartment emptied our bank accounts and increased our credit card balances. Everywhere we turned, someone wanted or needed money.

I began to think about what my friend had said about feng shui and the wealth corner. Could she be right? I bought some books and discovered it didn't have to be a live fish. Any sort of water symbol could provide what feng shui experts call a "cure."

Learning that flowing water is the next best thing to live fish, I placed a stone fountain in the corner where the goldfish tank used to be. Tiny rocks and shells decorated the gray slate, giving it a unique personality. A tiny fisherman sat on one of the larger stones, dangling his toothpick pole in the water to catch little plastic fish.

It couldn't replace Buddy's companionship, but as I worked at my computer every evening, sending out story pitches and trying to make connections with editors, the sound of the fountain became a comforting background noise.

One fountain grew into a water-themed collection taking up two shelves. Flowing crystal frames displayed seascape photos from our wedding on the beach. Pods of dolphin figurines cast a blue tinge against the white walls. Many of the trinkets were gifts from my sister who had learned about my "water corner" and knew I had always liked dolphins. A few held special meaning because I purchased them on vacation in meaningful locales—a ceramic ring of dolphins I picked up in the Florida Keys, a candleholder from Daytona Beach.

The cure wasn't dramatic. Instead of losing money, we began to break even. My freelance career became profitable as I generated a list of reliable clients. I found a new part-time job with less stress and more hours. At the end of each month, we even had a little bit of money left to tuck away. Things are looking up and, for the first time, the possibility of owning a home is not so far out of reach.

Wherever we go, a special spot in the southeast corner will be reserved for our elemental display. Every so often, I become aware of the sound of rushing water and smile in gratitude for the power of the ancient art of feng shui and the important role that water plays in our lives. All because of a fish named Buddy.

Midnight Tide

MICHELLE WALSH

From a young age, I was terrified of water. My parents spent many days at the beach trying to coax me into the ocean with children who were happily splashing. Every summer, my father bought arm floats, child surfboards, and other water toys in an effort to help me face my fears. I looked at the shiny new toys, but there was no convincing my child mind that the ocean wasn't going to eat me for dinner.

My fear prevented me from engaging in many activities with friends. On trips to the water slide, while all of my friends ecstatically slid and dived into the pool, I sat at the snack stand slurping frozen lemonade, wishing I could be with them.

On a school trip to Battleship Cove when I was eleven, I was excited to explore old boats—until I realized that the boats were on the water. For the first time, I decided to face my fears and get on the boat to explore with my friends and teachers.

As soon as I peered over the edge of the boat and saw the water below, I broke into tears. I began crying and hyperventilating and had to be carried off the boat by my history teacher. He sat at a picnic table with me while I cried.

"Gee whiz," he said. "For someone who is afraid of water, you're certainly making plenty of it yourself."

That made me laugh, but I still didn't get back on that boat.

The irony of my water fear is that I have lived on quite a few islands. I have not chosen to live on islands—it's just one of those things that keeps happening. I am always brought to the water.

My water fears were washed away about seven years ago. I was working on Block Island for the summer. I rarely went to the beach, and if I did, I sat as far away from the tide as possible.

One July night, I lay in bed, working myself into an emotional spiral. My mind was full of the universal questions. *What is my purpose? Where should I go? Where am I going to be ten years from now?* I was overcome by a feeling of hopelessness. Eventually, I got out of bed and decided to walk to the beach. It was well after midnight and I was the only person on the streets.

My mind raced as I walked to the beach in search of answers. I thought it was odd that I had the idea to go to the beach, since normally it was the last place I wanted to go. *Maybe the tide will just pull me out and that will be the end of me*, I thought.

I walked out along the beach and sat closer to the ocean than usual. The island was completely silent. All I could hear were the sounds of the ocean waves crashing as I breathed in the salty air and looked up at the full moon. The tide washed up and gently touched my feet and retreated back. I began to cry uncontrollably, but it wasn't the terrified cry from the fears of my youth. It was a cry of joy that seemed to come from somewhere both deep inside of myself and outside of myself. *This is so beautiful*, I thought, as tears cascaded down my face. My grandmother used to talk about "happy tears," and

I never knew exactly what she meant until that evening on the beach.

I continued to cry joyously as I watched the ocean inching closer to me. All of the fear I had toward her was stripped away in that moment. It was one of the most all-encompassing spiritual epiphanies I have ever had. I saw the ocean as female, as the universal mother, nurturer, and sustainer of life whose tides were guided by the moon. I knew that she had been trying to bring me home to her my whole life, yet she was patient, knowing I would come eventually. That first moment when she brushed up against my feet, it was as if I heard her say, "It's OK."

I stared at the rippling waves for what seemed like hours, then took off all of my clothes, letting them fall into a pile on the sand. I walked into the ocean until the water reached my waist, and stood looking at the moon as the tide pushed and pulled my body. I wasn't scared. I crouched down until the water reached my neck, still feeling the push and pull of waves on my skin. I felt safe there, as if I were standing in the center of the universe.

I knew something profound had happened. The ocean felt like an old friend who held me, when I wanted nothing more than to lie under the covers and cry tears of confusion and doubt. She didn't cling to me, as I had always feared. She held me softly in her waves and let me go when my shoulders grew cold, and I retreated to the shore.

A few weeks later, I packed up my belongings and headed to Manhattan, my next island. I took the Staten Island ferry, stood at the railing, and watched the water go by. Fear never crossed my mind.

The Lake

BOBBI PETTEY

I screwed up. I had slept in. Every morning during the week, I meet a friend to walk. Not this morning, though. Usually it is she who sleeps in, not I. I was angry at first for being so irresponsible. I really needed the walk, if not for the exercise, then for the "ear," the friendship.

It had been a tough few weeks preparing for the possible work interruption at the hospital. As a leader in the staffing department, I found it quite stressful balancing management, patient care, and our nursing relationships at the same time. I needed to talk. Missing that precious moment really bit.

As in most circumstances, however, if we embrace those times and breathe into life, those instances turn out to be some of our greatest gifts. It was 5:30 A.M. I decided to walk anyway. I needed the time to pray, think, meditate, and be. A time to feel the vision and lay out intentions.

I took my normal route along the concrete paths and suburban houses where most of my neighbors still slept. I continued on those hard paths as I worked my way toward the soft beauty of woods and water. As I approached the lake, I saw how still and reflective it looked. It beckoned me to sit and observe. It had a story to tell.

So I sat . . . and waited . . . waited for the story to appear. I didn't have any preconceived ideas, nor any notion as to what questions I needed answered.

Geese were honking wildly on the other side of the lake, while the lake itself was a perfect stillness. I noticed a dock across the lake just off to the left; it was calling, drawing me in. Blankets of green lawn lay on all sides. Willows gleamed and swayed gracefully, reflected in the mirror of the lake.

The dock was perfectly positioned off to the side . . . yet it was the center, the drawing force of the lake. It was there for those to come and rest their thoughts and fears, to find direction again.

Two families of ducks presented themselves from their protective reeds, as if to say, "Good morning, we know you are in a hurry. Just be patient, we'll tell it fast." The otter made two trips past, when usually he is only a one-pass kind of guy. A turtle hung in suspension, waiting and watching the activity of the lake.

The story comes to me. The noisy geese in the background remind me of the discontented nurses' union, constantly and incessantly vocalizing and positioning themselves for what appears to be an inevitable strike. Yet the lake, the hospital, stays still, not disturbed by the business and confusion of it all. The lake, though nudged here and there with slight disturbances, absorbs the energy, claiming all that come into its presence. Patients are taken care of and life goes on. The ducks, turtles, and otters are more present than ever. They are the support staff that keeps life going.

Interesting, I think to myself, how nature imitates life. Or is it the other way around? Not quite the story I had waited for, yet nonetheless here it was, offering itself to me. Interesting how the questions of life can be answered by simply slowing down to notice.

The lake is a mirror, not only for the landscape around it, but also for us to look into and out on, so that if we're still, we can see ourselves fully and truly. Not only who we are, but who we are to be. The world presents itself to us and waits for us to play our role.

"What role am I to play today?" I ask the lake.

It answers. "You are called to be the dock. You are called to be the center physically and spiritually. Calming, steadfast, reassuring that all will be well as it is and as it will be."

I walked back home, fully knowing who I was and whom I was called to be. So what happened? People rested on and in me. I was there when they needed me and even when they didn't. The potential strike was averted. I was the dock.

A Man of Water

JAMES McGRATH

I went to the lake this morning,
   the mountains rested
   in its liquid darkness.

I went to the lake this morning,
   I walked into it
   on long white aspen legs.

The lake was crowded with the silence
   of coots and yellow water lilies
   praising the calm.

I went to the lake this morning,
   a percolating man of water
   making the mountains and darkness quiver.

An Offering of Water

SHARON UPP

Endless mounds of charred and pockmarked lava rock, separated only by a thin line of highway, stretch in every direction on the Kona side of the Hawaii, the "Big Island." The blue Pacific crashes along the outer rim, cradling the peak of fire in soothing water. Thanksgiving is balmy. Days are windy and warm and evenings cool. Sloping toward the resort, jungle vegetation, tropical birds, and colorful flowers break through the lifeless terrain. The Pacific is calm and crystal clear, the sand black. A salty breeze cools the back of the neck. After three days of peace and relaxation, we head for Hilo.

Mountains covered in stands of bamboo, pine trees, eucalyptus, meadows, farms, homes with lanais, and small towns with "Old West" storefronts pass by as we travel inland toward Hilo. Hilo lies next to a deep port. An old-fashioned town, it retains only part of its past, the rest destroyed by the last tsunami. Early twentieth–century buildings line one side of the main street. The opposite is empty. The wave somehow crashed, jumped over the businesses still standing, and continued on its way. There are no plans to rebuild. The children, whose school is now in an old theater, have daily reminders of the devastation. The walls are lined with photos—evidence of a charming town resting precariously in impermanence.

We stay at the B&B owned by our son's friends Rick and Maria. Nestled on a hilltop overlooking the ocean, the place is serenaded by the pounding of the waves. It is pure bliss. The sun glistens in the water as the surfers patiently await their next ride.

People know one another. Main Street is friendly. Transplants bond and create alliances to offset the delicate balance between natives and mainlanders. Hawaiians are often wary. Open-air markets are fragrant with flowers and fresh bread. Canopies shade craft vendors, whose seashell necklaces are popular with the tourists. Elaborate tropical bouquets cost $5, including the ti leaf–wrapped bucket. Fresh ahi and mahi mahi are daily staples, along with papaya and mango. Sushi and cheeseburgers with fries coexist with fried eggs and rice in local restaurants.

Our son, Christopher, has moved here to be a glass blower and sell beautifully crafted sea creatures to islanders and tourists alike. His partner, Elisha, still has one foot on the mainland, but she's holding up admirably. Aja, Elisha's daughter, seems to take it all in stride. Our daughter Elise loves being lulled to sleep at night by the song of the Pacific. She and Aja enjoy the marketplace and shops on Main Street. As for me, let me snorkel for hours in the pristine waters. Sure, they're churned up a bit by a storm, but I won't let that stop me from entering. I love the great ocean and feel at home in her depths. The warm pools with an outlet to the sea are a favorite. Because of the temperature, I feel like swimming for hours. Colorful fish head toward hidden caves in the rocks as I pursue them with a camera.

Christopher has purchased some land that he wants us to see. We jump into the SUV and head toward the property, which includes a volcano and two waterfalls. How he manages to find the lot is a mystery to me. The streets seem mostly unmarked. Hawaiians give directions by saying, "You head toward the large mango tree . . ." Yet, he is at home and has no trouble finding the gate standing guard at a driveway surrounded by wild orchids and no fence. A gate with no fence strikes me as odd. He gets out to unlock it. *We could just walk around,* I think.

Pulling into the "driveway," we look around. Diminutive lavender orchids are suspended from pale green stalks in every direction. Treading the rocky ground requires equilibrium. I'm drawn to a spot to the left. My hands are directing me like a dowser's wand. They pulsate with energy. "Do you feel that?" I ask Elisha.

A clear vision arises . . . first steam, followed by a vibrant red stream of lava traveling underground. Elisha confirms that there is a lava tube underneath us. I stand fixed by the energy. I let the energy travel up and down. I sense the presence of ancient Hawaiians . . . three . . . two males and one female. They stand behind me. They feel supportive. They tell me, "This is no place to build anything permanent." I feel reverence. Their tone is caution, not menace.

I move to another spot toward the end of the driveway. Again, I'm told, "This is no place to build anything permanent."

I turn to Elisha. "If you build here, it won't last. You will lose your investment." She looks puzzled, but I know she believes me.

"Will you tell Christopher?" she asks.

I have to think about it. I know I must. Too often I have ignored my visions, my intuition and instinctive knowing. (On this very trip, I had a clear vision of our daughter missing her flight from Oahu. She did and she had to spend the night there before joining us the next day.)

How can I disappoint him? I think, but I know I must tell him. I call him over.

"Do you feel the energy of this place?"

He responds, "Yeah, sometimes it makes the hair on my arms stand up." He knows. That's part of why he wants to work here.

"Have you had the place blessed by a *Kahuna?*" I ask.

"No, not yet. We haven't found anyone."

"You must . . . before you proceed, even with a palapa hut. And you must bring an offering—fresh water and hibiscus flowers. You need to make an offering of fresh water. It's important."

I love the spirit of the Hawaiians who come to offer a well-intentioned warning. They do so with compassion. I want to spend time with them and bring them fresh water and flowers. I want to feel them at my back. They are strong, eternal, and completely honest.

As we pull away in the SUV heading for the waterfalls, I think about the two men and the woman who stood behind me for a moment. I can still feel their power. They remain with me, as does the island, an ancient ring of fire nestled in the cool blue waters of the Pacific.

A Pool of Water

MARGO FALLIS

I'd come to Scotland to find out who I was. My parents immigrated to the United States when I was a child and I'd never again seen my extended family. I grew up not knowing who I was or where I belonged. After years of saving money, I flew back to my homeland to find answers.

Early one morning, I looked out my window to find the mist hiding the hills. It swirled and floated across the land like a specter. I lifted the window for a better look. From the hidden hills came a low, mysterious voice. It called to me, beckoning me, hypnotizing me with an enchanting song. I'd heard tales of the Highland mist and its haunted illusions, but I knew there was a reason it called to me. I tossed a few things in my backpack, put on warm clothes and boots, and disappeared into the gauzy fog.

As the sun rose higher, the mist evaporated and I delighted in the scene before me. Green hills spread as far as I could see, dotted with patches of purple-blooming thistle. Sheep grazed and an occasional lamb frolicked through the heather. Billowy clouds with gray undersides looked as though they'd been painted against the azure sky by one of the great masters.

After hiking several miles, I left the hills behind and entered a dense wooded area. Ferns the height of an elephant hung between oaks, dangling their feathery leaves.

Bracken sprung from the ground, wrapping itself around fallen hollow tree trunks and carpeting the woodland floor in asparagus green. The smell of damp vegetation mingled with scent of the rich brown earth surrounded me and lured me deeper into the woods.

An eagle soared high above. It glided in circles. My eyes followed its every move. As I watched the eagle swoop low to the ground, something caught my attention. Curious, I pulled apart a mass of tangled sweet pea vines blocking my path. A cave, barely visible behind its doorway of blossoming rhododendron bushes and flowering gorse, invited my entry. I wedged myself between the wall of the cave and the foliage and squeezed into the darkness.

Here, the smells were different—musty and ancient. I sat down, my back pressed against the stone wall for support, and looked around. I visualized my ancestors, brave Pictish men and women, hiding in this cave, shivering in the oppressive dampness.

I rummaged through my backpack, pulled out a flashlight and a bag of trail mix, and found the courage to walk deeper into the cave. The beam of light shooting from the modern torch in my hand, cast an ethereal luminosity on the moss-coated walls.

Drops of clear water, pure and untouched after its fall from the heavens, trickled over the emerald moss and huddle around my boots. The water gathered in the indentations of the cave floor. When full, the droplets spilled over and ran across the slanted floor into the depths of darkness I had still yet to explore.

After walking another half an hour, a powerful surge of loneliness tinged with fear overcame me. My flashlight beam darted from wall to wall and from ceiling to floor. The sound of water, like a trickling brook, echoed from another part of the cave. I followed the lamenting sonance. Within minutes I stood next to the flowing water. It waltzed its way deeper into the cave. I shadowed the bubbling stream for a while, ending my sojourn in a pool of crystal fluid. Sparkles of silver shone as the beam of light brushed across the surface. I couldn't resist sipping the clear water. I lay down on my belly and dipped my cupped hands into the cool water, scooping some out. I drank and smiled as the icy liquid ran down my throat.

I noticed an object, glimmering and golden, that looked out of place lying at the bottom of the pool. I reached for it. The water came up to my shoulder as I stretched my grasp. I pulled out an auric chain from the depths. Dangling from the center a round medallion gleamed, carved with antiquated Celtic design. Drops of water snaked their way into the dimpled gold. It's surface turned lambent as a handful of lustrous diamonds.

I gazed in awe. Having a background in ancient Celtic design, I knew the value of this piece of work, carved by the refined fingers of a craftsman long ago. Delight filled my bosom as I thought that maybe one of my own forebears wore this medallion around his neck as he battled the Norsemen in a great war, or perhaps he'd owned many pieces like this, spoils of conflicts with the enemy. I slipped it into my pocket and lay down again, looking at my reflection in the still water.

A tingling sensation started in my toes and moved up through my body, coursing through my blood like a million butterflies in flight. At that instant I saw the medallion and its original owner mirrored in the water. His bronzed eyes, similar to my own, glowed with pride; his hair, dark and straight, cupped his strong jaw. His chest, muscular and sinewy, bulged with strength and might. The medallion hung around his neck and lay against his breast. A smile, small and meek, showed his courage and humility.

A tear fell from his eye. I reached out my hand to catch it. It landed in my palm. I held it and felt his love travel from the distant years into my soul. I held my hand high above the pool and let the tear slide off. In slow motion it cascaded, splattering against the watery mirror, sending a ring of tiny waves outward from its impact. The image disappeared. I turned and looked around me, but he no longer existed in my world. For just a moment, the pool had shared its magic with me. The image in the reflection is forever burned into my mind and my heart. The Celtic warrior was family. He was the reason for my very being. I am, because of him.

With deep reverence and humble countenance, I put the medallion into my backpack and made my way out of the cave. I found the answer to my origins in a pool of water hidden in a dark cave in the woodlands of northern Scotland. I knew I belonged.

Watery Wavelengths

MELISSA WADSWORTH

Water infuses my life; it is everywhere, even in my dreams. It provides radiance to my living landscapes gives voice to my inspirations, and speaks to my soul.

Most importantly, the gentle cleansing nature of water refreshes me, washing and soothing my body, mind, and soul. One day it did much more.

My friend Mary and I decided to get out of the city and take a road trip to a spa a few hours north of Los Angeles. The excursion included an invigorating bike ride. We began our ride in the cold mist of a foggy Ventura morning. At first we shivered in the salty spray as we rode inland toward Ojai. But no more than a mile into the ride, the air became dry and warm.

Soon the hot sun beamed upon us as we wove for miles along a path following escalating hills. We enjoyed the changing scenery and the exertion, our sweating bodies encouraged to push harder by the prospect of reaching our destination.

As we entered Ojai, the scent of orange blossoms sweetened the air. Fruit tree groves ran in rows in the valley, and palms and birds of paradise gave the illusion of an oasis respite.

The white stucco spa building was quiet and cool, shaded by tall eucalyptus trees. In the women's lounge area, two women were discussing the launch of a new body scrub, lowering their voices as we walked past. Another woman lolled in the Jacuzzi, eyes closed, head resting against the cool blue tile corner.

We showered and then let ourselves be enveloped by the warm, detoxifying steam of the sauna. Moisture escaped from my pores almost immediately, rivulets running down my forehead and throat, flowing from shoulders and muscled arms, saturating the round arch of my stomach. I breathed deeply, allowing myself to melt into the wetness, to center my awareness on the feeling of release in mind and body. I held a cold lemon-scented washcloth to my forehead and across the back of my neck to prolong my steam stay.

Twenty minutes later, I stepped out into the refreshing air and sat, towel-wrapped, for a few minutes in a white whicker chair, letting my body temperature cool down. Before long, I was unable to resist the lure of the Jacuzzi. I stepped into the hot water, allowing the water jets to massage my lower back, thighs, knees, and the bottoms of my feet. I was sweating again, feeling as though I was replenishing all bodily waters with each sip of ice-cold water. This was cleansing at a deep cellular level. A sense of healing and grace pervaded my senses.

By the time I got out of the Jacuzzi, all my energy was focused on wrapping my liquid limbs into the cozy comfort of a terry cloth robe. I saw an outdoor area with a fountain running down an adobe wall. Just two lounge chairs sat next to it, one occupied by a woman reading. I settled into the remaining chair, more content than I could ever remember being.

I closed my eyes, savoring the aroma of dry orange blossom air, as appreciative as a wine lover taking a deep waft of a bouquet. I listened to the fountain, its fluid cadence like a watery Om. I wanted to be nowhere else, wanted to go nowhere else. There was no schedule, no requirement but to experience the gratitude of being right where I was.

Suddenly, but without fanfare or disruption of my serenity, I heard soft static like an old radio being tuned in to a receptive station. Then three words sounded clearly in my head: "but she's asleep." It was like an angel whispering in my ear. I could feel my lips curve into a gentle smile, but I felt no need to open my eyes. I was utterly happy.

When I did open my eyes a few minutes later, the other woman was still quietly reading. Reluctantly, I got up from this sweet spot to see where my friend was. She was drying her hair in the locker room, so I stepped into the shower to wash the final remains of saltiness from my skin. I was so sure of my new knowledge, so satisfied by the truth of the experience that I didn't even feel the need to confirm the event with Mary immediately.

Once seated for dinner I asked her if she had spoken to the woman on the patio while I was resting. She said, "No, I was inside, looking at you and thinking, 'I want to let Mel know that I'm going to call Gary, *but she's asleep.*'" I joyfully told Mary that I had heard her thinking. She laughed in amazement.

The most astonishing thing about the entire incident was that it felt both completely normal and totally miraculous. All that water cleansing and relaxation at a cellular level, throughout the entirety of my being, had put me in a state so pure that there was not one single thought going through my mind. No musings, no needs or desires to consider—nothing but absolute contentment. I was an open vessel, receptive to thought waves, to hearing the universe.

Three little words gave me a glimpse into what we are capable of as humans, into the infinite power of a quiet mind. I mentioned this episode to an alternative health practitioner, who said that what made it especially amazing was that my ability to hear Mary thinking wasn't hindered by other people's thoughts and the other mind chatter that normally clutters the "airways."

All the elements converged that day at the spa to create an optimal atmosphere. All unnecessary components, our typical life toxins and noise in thought and body, had been broken down and washed away. Water had done its magical work. It's hard to imagine that I'll ever be able to duplicate this ideal state again, but I revel in the possibility.

Siren Call

VICTORIA NASH

The call came at dinnertime. I was fixing liver and onions.
When I answered the phone and heard the voice on the
other end say she was dead, had drowned, had floated off
to death in three feet of water, I thought, I haven't heard
this right. She could swim like the proverbial fish, this
flaxen-haired stepdaughter of mine. She was fourteen,
for God's sake. Fourteen-year-olds don't drown in three
feet of water so far away in some northern swimming
hole marked clearly "No swimming." Not here. Don't do
it here. Don't swim. Don't float. Don't go under. Don't
surrender. But, she did, there, in those Wisconsin Dells
so far her Ohio home.

"If only I hadn't bought her that new pink and white–
checked swimsuit," I said. That's it. It's my fault. It must
be my fault. I bought her the suit. I let her go. I wasn't
watching, wasn't there to tell her no, to reach out for her
when the water took her under and refused to give her
back, wasn't there to save her, to save me, to save us all.

Months came and went, but the pain didn't. It stayed
my constant companion. I went to work. I did the laundry. I cooked and cleaned and pretended to heal for my
husband's sake, but the wound was still raw. Time wasn't
doing its job.

"Come on," my friend Polly said. "Come to Lilydale
with me. It will be fun."

Fun. What a foreign notion. What an undeserved diversion for someone so burdened by guilt. No. Fun was not the selling point. It was the notion of getting away, of running away, that was appealing.

A few days later we piled into Polly's green Chrysler convertible, and off we went to visit the spiritualists, the soothsayers, and the healers in the land of the metaphysically fit.

We wandered the grounds, visiting gift shops and drinking in the sweet aromas of a rainy summer afternoon.

Then I saw it. I'd never been there before, but the old Victorian house looked familiar, welcoming. A simple sign above the door read "Medium." A woman stood in the doorway. She seemed to be waiting for someone.

"I can take you now," she said.

I suddenly realized she was speaking to me.

"Excuse me?" I said, not certain what she meant.

"You came to see me, didn't you?" she said. "Well, I can see you now."

She motioned me inside, indicating her fee was $20, but she wasn't going to charge me.

"I've been waiting for you. I have a message," she said.

At her coaxing, I sat on an overstuffed sofa across from her.

"You look confused," she said.

"I am. You don't know me, but you've been waiting for me?" I said, my brow curled in skepticism. "Bet you say that to all the passersby."

"No," she said, ignoring my sarcasm. "Only to the ones I've been waiting for."

I wondered at that moment what had possessed me to come into this stranger's house. How could I be so gullible as to be lured into this den of charlatanism?

I said nothing. I wasn't falling prey to this. Wasn't going to volunteer anything. I never met this woman, nor had my friend. I wasn't going to be trapped in her web. All these people read body language, see the need in people's eyes, and feed on the desperation of their pain, their sense of loss, their need to connect. No. Not me. I'm not giving it up so that I can be swindled.

I sat, stone-faced, an unwilling spectator at a con game. She didn't seem overly anxious to convert me, either. She offered no qualifications. Her environment was a simple living room. No crystal ball. No tarot cards. No tea leaves. She had a peaceful face capped by salt-and-pepper curls and looked like someone's grand-mother. She *was* someone's grandmother, and she was in no hurry. There was no clock ticking here, no rush to turn customers.

She sat back in her chair, smiling at me.

"I've seen her," she said.

"Seen who?"

"The girl. The young blond girl."

"What girl?" I asked.

"The girl in the shallow water. She's pretty. Beautiful bright blue eyes," she said.

I knew. I knew what girl she meant.

"She's all right, you know," she said. "She really is. It wasn't your fault. She wants you to know that. She wants you to know that it didn't hurt and that she's all right, but she wants you to be all right, too."

I felt my eyes welling up with tears—more water, the kind of water in which I had been drowning, the salt sea of tears. I couldn't speak. Couldn't ask how this could be, how this stranger could know without even knowing my name, without ever meeting me, without any living, breathing connective tissue between us.

"She wants you to know something else," the woman said, smiling now. "She still loves the water."

The woman got up from her chair, and patting my hand she said, "That's all. She just wanted me to tell you. Now go in peace."

I walked outside, outside where the afternoon had earlier been filled with rain, but where now the wind was full of summer smells and the sun had decided to shine for the first time all day.

As I passed underneath a tree at the edge of the woman's driveway, a single drop of rain fell from its damp canopy and came to rest gently on my cheek. Water. Pure, clear, crystalline water. Like tears. Like the body of some far-off swimming hole. The cleansing stuff of morning baths and spring showers. The power of Niagara and Victoria and the riptides. The blessed contents of the baptismal font. The sacred waters that wash over us in our mother's womb. The magic elixir of life.

The raindrop fell, freed from its captivity, and I knew I was free, too. We come from the water, and sometimes, unburdened, we go back.

Ocean of Tears

DIANE QUEEN MILLER

It was November in Montana and the long, cold winter had begun. Just for a lark, I called the travel agency and asked if there were any specials to Hawaii. Almost magically, they found a $367 roundtrip from my hometown!

I called Robert, an actor friend who lived on Maui, and he invited me to stay at his home. We had not seen each other for a couple years, and I looked forward to catching up on old times with him and sharing our mutual love for live theater and acting.

Robert and I had met during a transcontinental flight from New York to Salt Lake City. When I pulled out a script to work on my lines for "You Can't Take It with You," the connection was made. We talked the hours away about productions we had acted in, directed, or just loved watching.

Salt Lake City came too quickly. In the Salt Lake terminal, we checked the flight boards for our departure times. Mine had a two-hour delay, but his left right away. No time was left for us. He put down his luggage, took my chin gently in his hand, lightly kissed my cheek, and walked away.

Over the next couple years, we wrote, talked on the phone, mailed cassettes with our thoughts, and videoed theater productions. We sent funny cards with playbills and talked about getting together again.

Our days on Maui were filled with sunlight, rustling palms, warm beaches, drives to Hana, waterfalls, hand-woven palm baskets, a first taste of passion fruit, stinging wind-blown sand, and cloud formations that went on and on. It felt like we had been best friends all our lives, not two people meeting for the first time on a flight.

We talked, drove the island, cleaned his house on a rainy day, and each of us spent some time alone. The days had a pleasing rhythm of activity and rest, and I felt at peace.

A few days before my departure, Robert was having a restless morning and asked for my help. He was trying to let go of an area of his life that caused him constant emotional pain.

Taking his rusted, open-top Jeep to a breathtakingly beautiful, hidden bay away from the tourist sites, we found a place to sit on a sun-warmed lava shelf high above the ocean. When I walked to the edge I could see the waves breaking below us and hear them seconds later. We sat on the ledge facing each other, closer to the palm trees and away from the edge.

"I've hung on to this far too long," Robert said.

He talked of what had brought about the pain and how he wanted to let it go, finally and completely. As he worked through the healing process, I listened and silently prayed that the tears he was shedding would be washed away along with the pain.

At that moment, I looked up toward the edge of the shelf and saw a wave towering above us just about to break. Robert turned around as I gasped, and the water broke over the edge onto our rock. I watched as tiny droplets of water from the wave splashed upon his face, literally washing away the tears and taking them to the depths of the Pacific Ocean. Not a drop of seawater touched anywhere else on either of us.

We both sat very still, hardly daring to look at each other in case it had been a dream. When my shaking legs were steady enough, I walked to the edge and saw, once again, the waves far below us crashing against the lava walls and bursting into white and blue foam before pulling back to begin again.

Robert kept repeating, "It's gone," "It's going to be alright," and "Did that really happen?"

While we slowly walked back to the Jeep, I silently gave thanks to the Creator who would take time to listen to the prayers of a person in need and gently wash his tears away.

Wash Day

PATRICIA BRODIE

It is time to fill the washing machine,
add powerful soap.
This is the day we'll get everything clean.

At first it may seem like Monday's routine:
laundry bags bulging with soiled residue.
Yes, it's time to fill the washing machine.

We'll scrub out grime, stains, and crime,
grief, anomie, hypocrisy, too.
Today's the day we'll make everything clean,

eliminate poverty, leave forests green,
get rid of jealousy, greed, servitude.
Oh, it's time to fill the washing machine.

Abuse will be gone
alcohol, power
This is the day we'll get everything clean.

We'll launder out war, and all that's obscene,
wash harmony in love, happiness, truth.
It is time to fill the washing machine
for this is the day we'll get everything clean.

At Water's Edge

Lynn Robbins

That morning, at the very moment I pushed the computer's on-button, something at the river gave a call to come see. The call felt genuine, not just avoidance of the work at hand, so I grabbed the camera and left the computer whirring.

Just a grassy 300 yards away, the Little Miami River lives up to its name—only waist-deep much of the year and narrow enough to talk across, throw a rock across. Life here is of a size I can hold, though the beauty often overwhelms me—little river, big beauty, huge joy.

The day was sparkling, sun not quite over the hill as I snuck my way down, purposefully sidestepping crisp leaves and twigs that might snap and scare off wary critters. I stepped carefully but hurriedly down the soft sand bank, wishing my eyes were on the sides of my head so I could see both upstream and downstream at once.

I spotted her right off, the one I'd hoped for, the Great Blue Heron, to the left, not far upstream, maybe fifty feet away. She was standing thin and proud in the shallows, her right eye already on me, her knees bending to take flight, her wings already unfolding and spreading before I could take her all in. So shy. She flew low upstream, and I crouched below branches to click her picture.

As I squatted there by the river, there came another wide-winged bird curving up to a bare sycamore branch above the rapids, flashing its fabulous white belly boldly against the hill. Osprey! First sighting this year, though one visits here each fall.

Now, without a focus, I took it all in, the big picture: the smell of wood smoke from a riverside gathering downstream; the totally enmeshed buzz of a million bugs; the rising sun spilling over the hill, making silver streaks on the water, shining on slick rocks at water's edge; cool air that had quickly gone warm.

I moved farther upstream to a place I've dubbed The Wash, a spot where high water has so many times slid around a higher stretch of bank that its path has washed a thirty-foot-wide gully down six feet to bare rocks.

I sat at its mouth, in a spot so low I was almost even with the river's rippling surface. With legs outstretched, feet just a foot from flowing water, and sun halfway up my right shoulder, again I surveyed my world. The river-length hill across the way was barely kissed with fall color, autumn's reds and yellows starting to push out the green, the long island in front of me fringed with gold.

And the water flowed: ripples to my left, rushing to my right, gurgles and bubbles and foam-dabbed crests everywhere. That age-old insistence intrigues me, water running forever to the sea, only to evaporate and return as rain next spring, to fill again the river's valley, flow again, gurgle again—not unlike my own leaving and returning and gurgling.

Life is so sweet there, the river forever teaching me life lessons—like how to keep moving, no matter what, and how not to take a flood, or a drought, too seriously. Time and again, as I watch the water go up and down, from blue to brown, I have learned that expectations are not only useless, they get in the way of seeing things as they are, and, at least at the river, "things as they are" couldn't be better.

The beauty around me is astounding, when I let myself see it, feel it, when I answer the call to come see, go look. And when I sit down low beside the river and let my nerves unjangle, feeding for even a minute or two on quiet, I find myself happier and more at peace than I have ever dreamed.

My southwest-Ohio little-river valley suddenly becomes a Colorado Rocky Mountain stream, Canadian backwoods waterway, Florida inland canal. I remember them all, love them all. But in that moment that one autumn morning, I saw the river as though I'd never seen it before, for it was not just the Little Miami River, not even just "my" river; it was *all* rivers, all rain, all water, and the oneness of that was—and remains—joyfully mind-boggling.

Soft-eyed and smiling, as I finally headed back toward the house, I stopped and turned, looking back at the river. In those few daydream seconds, I imagined myself pitching a tent there, on the riverbank, not just to camp for a day or two, but to live there year-round so I wouldn't miss anything, the river's call answered once and for all and for always.

But now, back at my desk, I know that, in truth, I live there already, no tent needed, my heart and soul forever a part of that glistening ribbon, the ocean, the rain, ready to water my neighbor's garden and drip on her head come spring.

Fins in the Water!

JUDITH DIANA WINSTON

Water has always been my friend. I played in it as a child every summer at my grandparents' cottage on Lake Michigan and spent part of every winter swimming in the warm Atlantic waters off the southeastern coast of Florida. Water was my home, my haven, the place I went when other things in life became too complicated. Even swimming a couple of laps in a pool was an instant de-stressor.

Now, I was battling for my life as the stormy water carried me farther and farther away from our luxurious sailboat. How could I have been so foolish?

We had been anchored three hours off of Grand Bahama Island on the shallow sand banks of White Sand Ridge, where the twenty-five-foot deep water harbored an indigenous pod of Atlantic spotted dolphins. We had been there for two days hoping to swim with them. Our schedule was to stay for another five, when Captain Michael suddenly announced that we were heading in.

"There's a storm headed our way and soon it will be too strong," he said. "I can't chance it." A collective groan arose from all eight of us dolphin enthusiasts. We were more than disappointed; we were devastated! We had seen the pod in the turquoise shallows our first day out and had quickly donned snorkels, masks, and fins and jumped right in. But the dolphins had other things to do that day. Although we tried to entertain them, they swam on, apparently not in the mood to play.

Earlier that day we'd been hailed by another boat in the area whose captain said they'd seen the pod some two miles away. Although I personally began to feel a bit like a stalker, we went anyway. No luck!

Now, although there were no dolphins, I'd asked Captain Michael for one last dunk before we left. "OK," he said. "But be quick about it and stay close to the anchor line," he advised. "That water's starting to get choppy."

I put on my snorkel, mask, and fins and jumped in. After all, water's always been my friend. It's like one big bathtub to me. Then I heard someone yell, "Fins in the water!" That's the way my friends and I identified the presence of dolphins in our midst, by the sighting of the large curved dorsal fin on their backs.

I let go of the anchor line and swam out a bit. I saw one of the dolphins breach, jump gracefully out of the water and back in again, so I swam out a bit farther. I lost all track of time and space and let the water carry me. Who cared about boats when there were dolphins to be met!

Unexpectedly, I was surrounded by three bottle-nose dolphins, two large ones and a baby. I could feel them slow down to keep pace with me. You know that if you are swimming in sync with dolphins, it's no accident. They're fast, and if you are keeping up, it's certainly not by chance.

The small one was clearly a baby and I felt the mother was showing him off to me, or vice versa. She nudged him toward me and he touched his rostrum—the part that looks like an elongated nose with the "smile" under-neath—to my shoulder. It felt like rubbery silk. I was in heaven. The third dolphin, a female, watched from the sidelines like a protective aunt.

Suddenly, I took a gulp of salt water and realized that the water was not choppy; it was downright wavy. I looked up. The boat seemed a long way off. I could see Captain Michael waving at me. In that instant, the water didn't feel so friendly anymore. Now, I felt like an alien and I began to panic. The harder I swam the more water I swallowed, until I started to gag.

"Be calm," I told myself. "You know water."

I took the snorkel from my mouth, slowed my pace and tried to become one with the water, to synchronize my breaststroke with the oncoming waves. But it was too late; I was too far out. I was still being pulled farther away from the boat. I silently prayed to Poseidon, Master of the Seas.

"Spare me, I've been a foolish child, but I can learn," I pleaded. "If you allow me to live, I will be your emissary, your servant. Never more will I take your power for granted."

I imagined my end, a fitting death. "Taken by the water she so loved," my friends and family would say. "Ironic that the thing she held so dear would take her from us!"

I wasn't prepared to go. Not now, not yet! Then, I felt myself go under. Everything grew dark and quiet except for the distant splashing of water and the buzzing and clicking of the dolphins' sonars. Suddenly I felt a nudge on my backside, then another! I came up and took a big gulp of air.

Unbelievably, the two adult dolphins were pushing me toward the boat. They were big (about six feet long) and strong, but they were gentle with me. They pushed and prodded while I swam, until I made contact with the anchor line, the baby swimming at my side. He gave me one last poke and they darted off.

I used the line to pull my exhausted body to the boat. The captain and my friends hauled me up dripping and shaking. Someone plopped a rubber parka on me as the rain started to come down. The captain turned on the motor and we began moving quickly. We put on life vests and lashed ourselves to our seats, the water from the bow's wake joining the downpour from the heavens as we began our arduous journey toward land. We all sat topside. It was sick-making to go below. It was a hard ride back, but I continued my prayers of gratitude.

I learned a powerful lesson that day. Water is fun to play in. Turquoise waters and white sand beaches are still my favorite places to be. But water is an elemental force of nature. It is alive and powerful. In a match of wills, I will always lose. Water demands respect, and it certainly has mine. I was extended grace that day and I won't forget it.

As for the dolphins—great and mystical creatures of the deep—I owe my life to them!

I formed a bond with the dolphins that will take at least a lifetime to explore. While with them, I felt I was in the presence of an intelligence that matched or exceeded my own. Their grace and power still fills my dreams.

Waves of Inspiration

MAUREEN MILLER-KNIGHT

I had just quit the worst job of my life and resolved to take a sabbatical to my favorite place of comfort—the Atlantic Ocean.

I placed a "For Sale" sign in my snow-filled yard and convinced myself that I deserved to enjoy the next three months worry free. I relished the thought of soul searching what I really wanted out of life. I planned to walk on sunny beaches, sit under palm trees, write in my journal, and enjoy balmy, tropical breezes.

Every day I set up my blue and white–striped umbrella and beach chair, stared out into the vast ocean, breathed deeply, and let the overwhelming sense of serenity engulf me. Then I pulled my journal out and wrote about life, love, people, dreams, and hope.

I lost all sense of time and place as I experienced the healing power of my friend, the sea. I sat on the sand in front of the tall grass and gazed into the waves, trying to let go of past frustrations and find the way to future happiness. Every day at this spot I prayed, listened to the soothing music of the waves receding over small pebbles, and watched the waves chase sandpipers seeking food in the sand.

It occurred to me how much I was like those birds. I ran through life searching for something to satisfy me— running along the same path, dodging waves, moving farther down the same path and running again. Where was I going? What was I running from?

These questions haunted me as each day I walked farther down the beach, attempting to reach the lighthouse in the distance.

I became aware of subtle differences in the ocean as I returned later and later, the tide coming in at higher levels to my sanctuary. The jagged rocks I easily walked in front of on the way were battered by ocean waves on the way back. Should I fight the waves and continue on my current course or venture around the rocks into new territory?

At first I stayed on the same path, fighting the thigh-high waves each day. Then one day I went around the rocks and found the most amazingly warm, soft beach sand.

Once again, the magical blue water enlightened me. I had been fighting my way along the same old path for many years; it was so familiar and comfortable that I continued on that unfortunate course, never looking up long enough to see the smoother route nearby. It was my epiphany, and I returned to Minnesota with a renewed confidence and commitment to quality of life.

Within six months, I had a rewarding job and was dating a wonderful man. Not just any man, but the right one. He wasn't like anyone I had dated before, because I kept taking the hard way, leading myself down rough roads over and over again.

When we met, I felt a sign from the mystical ocean as I placed my hand in my jacket pocket and found the smooth shell I had picked off the beach as a reminder to take the smooth path and search for quality of life. Almost instantly, I knew he was the smooth sand I had been searching for all along.

The Great Universal Solvent

JASON THOMAS GOMEZ

Scientists call water "the universal solvent." Given the spiritual encounter I had with it, I am inclined to agree.

It was the beginning of the river-rafting season. My wife, Angela, her sister, and I were about to ride the river for the very first time. Excited and elated to participate in such an exhilarating sport, we purchased a package for the entire weekend that included lodging, meals, and two days of guided tours down the American River. After learning the necessary safety requirements we thought we'd never need to know, we were on our way.

The first day went well. The second day brought a tougher ride, which took us through at least three turbulent rapids. As we lazed in the slow moving currents before approaching the final rapid of the trip, our guide invited those frisky enough to do so to jump in and enjoy the water.

My wife's adventurous side took hold of her. Being the concerned husband that I am, I jumped in after her, followed by another patron on our ten-person raft.

As Angela and I held hands in the water, floating downstream, we gazed into each other's eyes to let our souls meet and dance for a spell. We told each other that we loved each other, with the kind of romantic emotion that's seen in movies when two lovers are saying it for the last time.

Letting her hand go, as if to say, "I release you as a separate and free child of God to live life and experience it freely," I saw her drift away as I gained momentum. The river took its time bringing her downriver while I forged ahead.

Just then, I heard a cry farther downstream. It was the other patron who had floated ahead; he had hit a boulder and busted his shin. He tried to warn me of the oncoming rock. By the time I made out what he was yelling, I had hit the boulder and popped out. I began to shout at my wife who was innocently floating downriver without a clue about what lay ahead.

I saw her body pitch forward over the rock and not pop out. I continued downriver in what seemed like an eternal dead silence as I began to panic. Half a minute went by and Angela had not surfaced. I swam frantically and ignorantly upstream without success. After tiring myself out, I propped myself up on a rock and begin screaming at our boat, "Watch out for my wife, she's under the rock!"

They were on course to go right over the boulder and my wife as well. I feared she would be knocked unconscious by the raft. The entire crew sensed something was wrong by the bloodcurdling tone of my scream. They steered around the rock.

Angela had now surfaced, but she was caught in the back current of the river against the rock and couldn't get free. Bobbing frantically up and down, she flailed her arms about, gasping for air. What I thought was our last chance to save her failed as her sister reached out for her and missed grabbing her hand by inches.

My sister-in-law begged the guide to get out the raft and do something to save her sister. I recalled the last words that I said to my wife and wondered just how I would explain to her parents what happened on the river if she didn't make it. The complete and utter helplessness I felt is almost indescribable. I thought I could save her, I tried to save her, but it seemed it wasn't meant to be. At that moment I realized just exactly who, or what, was in control of life.

I had always thought I was in control of my life and that my choices and preferences made life what it was, but it was on this day, the day I thought I would lose my wife to Mother Nature, that I understood my place in the grand scheme of things.

The sheer emotional terror and spiritual anxiety I felt was enough to make me want to leave the safety of my rock join her. But I did not. I stood stern and steadfast and began to pray to the Creator for mercy and compassion on my simple human existence and that of my beautiful bride.

I felt a shimmer of hope as the bewildered guide hurriedly made his way out of the raft. He jumped out, leaving the rope in the raft as it floated past me downriver with patrons inside. In his haste, the one tool he took to save my wife, an oar, had been knocked loose from his grip by the rushing current.

He now stood just inches away from my drowning wife with no aid or tool in hand to save her. She was truly alone. "It wasn't until I saw our guide just standing there that I realized this is really it and began to make my peace," my wife later recalled.

The entire ordeal lasted only a short time, but seemed like an eternity to those of us on the river that day. All hope faded as the universe unfolded its illusion-breaking design.

At that moment, a small miracle took place. The very next raft to float down the river was a whitewater river rescue boat, complete with a team practicing for river emergencies.

What are the chances that in a river with no cell phones or walkie-talkies nearby that a rescue team would be there?

They pulled over to the side and got a rope ready to throw out. It was then that the river and Mother Nature surprised us all. As the rescue team threw out the rope to lasso it around Angela, the river let her go. No sooner had the rope hit the water than the current released her and she was pulled to safety—shaken, cut, and bruised, but alive.

She was given medical assistance, bandaged, and reunited with her sister and me. We greeted each other with tearful hugs, as we all realized we had almost lost her.

We did not go through the last rapid that day, but we did go back to that same river one year later, and my wife faced her fear with courage and confidence, knowing that no matter what happened she would be a willing participant in life.

We all learned valuable lessons that day. We learned how special and precious life truly is, and no matter how much we believe we're the end-all, be-all of our own lives, there are certain life currents that we cannot fight or control, only flow with. I was no longer going to fight the currents of my life.

That day, water, the universal solvent, dissolved my illusion of being in total and complete control. I hope my story serves as a reminder of the beauty of life and love and encourages everyone to dive right on into the river of life and see where it takes you.

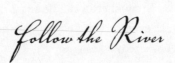

Follow the River

NANCY LOU CANYON

I am not afraid of storms for I have learned how to sail my ship.

—LOUISA MAY ALCOTT

Three years ago, I repeatedly dreamed of crashing waves washing me under and out to sea. Almost nightly I'd gasp awake in the dark, having barely escaped the roiling water of my dreams. At fifty, with a daughter and three stepchildren raised and on their own, I found my job as a mother downsized. My other job, bookkeeping at my husband's chiropractic office, had become a thorn in my side. It wasn't a good fit and I was doing it out of duty, not love.

I needed time alone to find myself. I needed quiet writing time to finish my book, *Whispering, Idaho*. I needed to make a commitment to my writing life and myself. I decided on a month-long retreat. This meant saying goodbye to my husband, my garden, art studio, pets, and friends. Would they all still be there when I got back? Would they still love me if I wasn't so available?

Then I had another dream. While packing for a bike trip, a sage woman spread a map across the floor. She drew a finger along a watercourse, advising me to follow the river instead of the mountains. I interpreted the dream to mean I had to follow my heart, the river, and not the cultural bias of what marriage or work should be. Also, I took it to mean I should choose my retreat closer to home instead of traveling southwest to the mountains. I found a little place by the Spokane River and packed up my car.

I arrived at the cabin with a borrowed laptop, art supplies, summer clothes, journal, tarot cards, and a bicycle. The first thing I did was walk out onto the deck where, a mere twenty feet north, the river rolled past, smelling of willows, fish, mud, and bull pine. Clutching the railing, I can still remember the pull—the water's immense power drawing me toward it. My dream was alive. I was both shaken and overwhelmed with relief. The first night, curled in bed in a room overlooking the water, I tingled with fear. The volume of water surging past was awesome. Everything vibrated with its thundering presence, including the bed.

My prayers were fierce. I wanted my fear to vanish. It only increased: fear of being alone, of the water, of intruders. I prayed to be kept safe, to live through the night. When my fear reached terror stage, my guide appeared in a chair at the foot of the bed. He was tall, bearded, gentle. His hands rested upturned in his lap. He told me he would watch over me during the night. Then a feminine presence appeared and wrapped me in milky veils.

My fear fell away. I was a child carried in my grandmother's arms. I fell asleep and dreamt of chattering water, liquid voices discussing my situation, encouraging me to let go and trust the universe.

As the month progressed and my long-held terror waxed and waned, sloughing off in tears, pacing, praying, and smudging, the river continued its journey toward the sea. Its calm surface reflected the clouds and trees; an occasional curl of current went rolling by, popping and laughing.

After each morning of writing, I ate my lunch and took a long walk, following footpaths dotted with black-eyed susan and sage. Merganser ducks drifted downstream, paddled back up, and floated down again. Gulls picked on the osprey couple nesting across the river; cliff swallows swooped at hatching bugs. I sketched the midday reflections of branches cast across the water's surface. Each day the water lowered a bit and the danger level lessened, and so did my fear.

At night, I beaded bracelets, listened to music, crocheted, took long baths, and chatted with my husband on the telephone. The orange glow of sunsets tinted the river and the west sides of the towering bull pines. Always the whooshing of the river accompanied my activities, and the weight of the passing water steadied me.

I learned from the river to respect my own rhythms. My time was freed up by not having to answer to anyone, and I relaxed into a natural schedule. I began to sleep better, to eat better, and to desire gentle exercise. I understood that at the root of my terror was a fear of abandonment. I knew I'd have to stick with my heart concerning my work schedule once back home. I also knew that the people in my life loved me and would support my movement forward, my choices for my life.

At the same time, I realized that instinctual fear served a purpose. My instincts informed me when I was in danger and when I needed to remove myself from a situation. As an adult, being constantly fearful was a leftover behavior from growing up with an abuser. This old fear was keeping me trapped in the *fight or flight* response.

Knowing that I was safe allowed me relax and to stay present with my life.

The river taught me through its natural sequence. First swift and dangerous, its dark undercurrents smothered beneath a green swollen surface. When the water began to drop, bent willow stems appeared, jumping about in the streaming water. Then lower still and willow whips rose up from the surface and leafed out, dancing stems in the current. Then bottom rocks appeared, mottled rusts and yellows, and were passed over unnoticed by laughing weekend rafters.

My dreams of crashing waves vanished. I came home and quit my bookkeeping job. I set my writing schedule, and with much of my book rewritten and the qualities of a *Blue River* meandering through *Whispering, Idaho* pinned down, I began a new book, *Stealing Time*. The sage woman pointed the way: follow the river.

Meditation:

WATER AND DREAMS

Nearly everyone has dreamed of water in one form or another. What does water mean when it shows up in your dreams?

Although interpretations vary, most dream interpreters agree that water is an important and powerful symbol. It can represent the fluid, unconscious mind and its shifting emotions. It can be a deeply spiritual symbol. It can also have sexual connotations. Exact meanings will differ depending on the type of water, the state of the water, and the dreamer's emotional state in connection with the water. Below are a few examples of what water can represent.

- ~ Clear water can be a sign of abundance, spiritual clarity, or good fortune. A large body of water that is calm and clear reflects "smooth sailing."

- ~ Murky or dirty water can be a sign of an uncertain emotional state, or a warning of troubled times ahead.

- ~ A waterfall can be a sign of refreshing cleansing. If it's a tumultuous waterfall, however, it can be a sign that you're feeling "out of control" on a subconscious emotional level.

- ~ Waves in your dream can mean anything, from peace and tranquility to emotional upheaval. How you react to the waves may reflect how anxious or stressful your life is.

~ Running water can be a predictor of wealth or happiness—unless someone else is in charge of the water (someone's hand on a faucet, for example) in ways that make the dreamer feel powerless.

~ Water in dreams can also represent the feminine principle and is often associated with birth—perhaps the birth of new ideas, opportunities, or creativity.

~ Dreams of drowning—either yourself or someone else—are usually the subconscious mind's way of communicating feeling overwhelmed, distressed, or worried about something. They rarely have a literal connotation, but it's important to pay attention to what they could be pointing to in your waking life.

How do you make the correct interpretation of water in your dreams? Trust your intuitive voice to guide you. First, write down a literal description of the dream as soon as you can after waking.

Recall as many scenes as possible. Describe in detail the water in the dream: Was it rough? Smooth? Vast and oceanic? Moving or still? Where were you in relation to the water?

Pay attention to your emotional dream state as you replay the dream in your mind, and write down what you felt.

Finally, view the water as a separate "character" in the dream. Still writing, ask the water what it wants from you, what message it has for you, why it appeared. If the meaning of the dream is clear by now, write down what you think it is.

If the meaning is not clear, at this point you have a choice. You can meditate for a few minutes and see what further guidance comes. Don't think about the dream as you meditate; instead, relax and clear your mind of all thoughts. At the end of your meditation, write down any further insights.

Another option is to wait until bedtime and ask your subconscious to give you another dream that clarifies the meaning of water in your first dream.

A third option is to wait a few days, then reread what you wrote in your dream journal. Sometimes, on rereading what you wrote, the meaning will be quite clear.

Contributors

Dawn Allcot is the editor of *Paintball Sports International Magazine*. She is a freelance writer whose work has appeared in such magazines as *Church Production*, *Sound & Communications*, and *School Band & Orchestra*, as well as on Web sites such as *www.absolutewrite.com*. Her story "A Plane Ticket, a Phone Call and a Country Song" appears in the *Cup of Comfort for Sisters* anthology. Dawn lives on Long Island with her husband and three cats. Contact her at *www.DawnAllcot.com*.

Stephanie Rose Hunt Bird is the author of *Sticks, Stones, Roots and Bones; Hoodoo, Mojo and Conjuring with Herbs; A Walkabout Home;* and *Motherland Herbal*. Her prose appears in the anthology *Age Ain't Nothin' But a Number: Black Women Explore Mid-Life* and the magazines *Natural Home*, *Herb Quarterly*, and *Sage Woman*. Bird taught painting at the School of the Art Institute of Chicago for many years. Her art can be seen on the Web site *www.stephanierosebird.womanmade.net*.

Patricia Brodie is a clinical social worker with a private psychotherapy practice in Concord, Massachusetts. Her poems have appeared in *The Edge City Review*, *Poetry Motel*, *California Quarterly*, *Poetry East*, *Möbius*, *Nanny Fanny*, *The Raintown Review*, *Colere*, *Ellipsis*, and other publications, as well as many anthologies. She recently won an honorable mention in a contest sponsored by the New England Poetry Club. Contact her at *patbr@gis.net*.

W. K. Buckley teaches at Indiana University (Northwest). He is editor of *Critical Essays on Louis-Ferdinand*

Celine and *New Perspectives on the Closing of the American Mind*, and author of *Lady Chatterley's Lover: Loss and Hope*. His chapbook *By the Horses Before the Rains* won the 1997 "Best Chapbook of the Year" from *Modern Poetry*. His latest chapbooks are called *Lost Heartland's Found* and *Denver Green and Taos Red*. Contact him at *wbuckley@iun.edu*.

Susan Carman is a grant writer and development professional. She writes poetry, essays, and short stories. Her work has appeared in publications including *Mid-America Poetry Review*, *Potpourri*, and *Catholic Digest*. She is a poetry editor and board member for Whispering Prairie Press. She strives to recognize the sacred in unexpected places each day.

Nancy Lou Canyon's poems, short stories, essays, and paintings have been published by Bainbridge Island Arts and Humanities Council's *Poetry Corners*, *Byline Calendar 2005*, *Poesy Magazine*, and *Spindrift*, and her poetry has also appeared on the Web site *www.poetsagainstthewar.org*. She has completed two novels, *Whispering, Idaho* and *Stealing Time*. She lives on Washington State's Kitsap Peninsula with her husband and two cats, and works in a studio overlooking the shipping lanes of Puget Sound. Contact her at *www.nancycanyon.com*.

Miki Onianya Conn, artist, storyteller, and poet, is executive director of the Hamilton Hill Arts Center, an inner-city center focused on the arts and culture of the African Diaspora. She teaches art to children and adults and facilitates workshops in creativity and spirituality.

Miki also curates exhibits and produces exhibition catalogs of black artists. An initiated priestess in the Yoruba tradition, Miki has recently focused her creative energies on writing. Contact her at *Mikiconn2@aol.com*.

Anne Coray lives at her birthplace on remote Qizhjeh Vena (Lake Clark) in southwest Alaska. Her work has appeared in *Green Mountains Review*, *The Southern Review*, *The Women's Review of Books*, and *Northwest Review*, among others. She has three chapbooks, including *Ivory* and *Soon the Wind*. Contact her at *northshoreink@gci.net*.

Kate Corbett is a freelance writer who lives in New England. She loves to write about and share her passion for the ocean and nature. She is currently working on several short stories. Contact her at *kcorbett_04@hotmail.com*.

Peggy Eastman is award-winning author of *Godly Glimpses: Discoveries of the Love That Heals*, and editor of *Share* magazine, a spiritual quarterly published by the Catholic Daughters of the Americas. Her work, including her poetry, has appeared in national publications such as *Guideposts*, *Ladies Home Journal*, *SELF*, *Working Mother*, and the *AARP Bulletin*. Contact her at *peggyeastman@cs.com* or visit her Web site *www.bookviews.com/BookPage/godlyglimpses.html*.

Karl Elder, author of five poetry collections, including *Phobophobia*, *A Man in Pieces*, and *The Geocryptogrammatist's Pocket Compendium of the United States*, is Lakeland College's Fessler Professor of Creative Writing and Poet in Residence. Among his honors are a Pushcart Prize, the Lucien Stryk Award, grants from the Illinois Arts Council for poetry and fiction, and Lakeland's Outstanding Teacher Award. For more than two decades, Elder has edited the magazine *Seems*. Contact him at *www1.lakeland.edu/seems*.

Marcia Fairbanks, a Piscean, writes in a room that faces the sea. Her work has been published in *Northeast Corridor*, *Contemporary Haibun*, *Tampa Review*, *Flashquake*, and other journals. Marcia is a Pushcart Prize nominee. She also edits and proofreads the work of others. Her e-mail address is *marciafair@comcast.net*.

Margo Fallis, born in Edinburgh, Scotland, has a lust for adventure and has spent most of her life traveling. When she's not exploring the world, she's writing about her experiences. Margo studies world history and ancient cultures, is teaching herself to read and write Chinese, and does watercolor and drawing. Married and mother of five children, Margo writes children's stories for her seven grandchildren. Contact her at *margofallis@yahoo.com*.

David Feela is a poet, freelance writer, writing instructor, book collector, and thrift-store pirate. His work has appeared in publications including *High Country News*, *Mountain Gazette*, *The Denver Post*, and *Yankee*, as well as in many anthologies. He is a contributing editor and columnist for *Inside/Outside Southwest*. His chapbook *Thought Experiments* won the Southwest Poet Series. Contact him at *feelasophy@yahoo.com*.

Charles Adés Fishman is director of the Distinguished Speakers Program at Farmingdale State University, associate editor of *The Drunken Boat*, and poetry editor of *New Works Review*. His books include *Mortal Companions*, *The Firewalkers*, and *The Death Mazurka*, nominated for the 1990 Pulitzer Prize. His fifth book, *Country of Memory*, as well as his tenth chapbook, *5,000 Bells*, were both published in 2004. Contact him at *carolus@optonline.net*.

Virginia Fortner is an educational consultant, teacher for homebound programs, adjunct professor for special education at several metropolitan colleges, and guide for Footprints, a study-travel experience. She does watercolors. Most of her published work has been informational, but writing poetry and fiction brings her true joy.

Barbara A. Gates, M.Div., is a hospice chaplain and United Church of Christ minister with a background in interpersonal relations, public speaking, analysis, counseling, and writing. Through her work, and as parent to former Columbine students, she has seen heartfelt care encourage emotional healing and create connections. She believes that if we tap in to our common humanity, our diversity can strengthen us. Barbara and her husband have two college-age children and live in Littleton, Colorado. Contact her at *bg@barbaragates.net*.

Jason Thomas Gomez defied conventional wisdom by switching his business major to comparative religion after a life-altering epiphany forever changed his evangelical perspective toward pluralistic ideals. Graduating from Cal-State Fullerton, he currently co-chairs the Religious Diversity Forum in Orange County, California, and is an active leader in Be The

Cause, a nonprofit organization. He is pursuing an M.A. in theology to usher in "the Age of Religious Reconciliation." Contact him at *jaag@earthlink.net*.

Lisa Waterman Gray's nonfiction has appeared in *GRIT*, *Mountain Living*, *The Kansas City Star*, *The Business Journal*, *Kansas City Nursing News*, *Kansas City Magazine*, *Kansas City Homes & Gardens*, *The Pitch*, and *The Sun*. She received a President's Award for Outstanding Journalism from the Kansas City Press Club. *The Kansas City Star*, *Potpourri*, and *Kansas State Poetry Society* have published her creative work. Contact her at *grays4@planetkc.com*.

Bill Grover is a passionate supporter of personal transformation—his own and others'. He invites inquiry into all the hidden corners of life and delights in assisting others in this process. He commutes between his home in Florida and a community house in the Midwest. Contact him at *billgrover@usa.net*.

Susan Elizabeth Hale is a singer, poet, and music therapist. She is author of *Song and Silence: Voicing the Soul* and *Sacred Space—Sacred Sound*. Susan teaches workshops and classes throughout the United States, Great Britain, and Canada, and she directs The Voice of the Rose: Songkeeper Apprenticeship Program in Taos, New Mexico. Contact her at *www.angelfire.com/nm/susong* or *susong@yahoo.com*.

Pat Hartman, former banker and financial officer, is an artist and author. She lives in the Midwest with her husband, Jim, and has two children and three grandchildren. She believes that faith and science must work together and that you must grow, change, and forgive. She says, "Don't let anyone take your hope away."

Sherry Norman Horbatenko lives in southeast Georgia in a small town of milk and honey called Woodbine. She shares her life with two paperweights (who greatly resemble cats) and her mother. She tutors, maintains a small farm, a home business, and two rental properties. She has written short stories and a fantasy novel, with two sequels in process. She's looking for a good agent who will take her work and help "make it happen." Contact her at *horbaten@gate.net*.

Nancy Jackson is a writer of both light and dark, always striving to find a balance. Her works can be seen both online and in print, including stories, essays, articles, and poetry. Some of her work can be found at *Twilight Times*, *Romancing the Soul*, *Waxing and Waning*, *Love and Lost Love*, and *Literati*. For darker works, see her Web site at *www.nancyajackson.com*.

Judith Bader Jones grew up on the banks of the Mississippi River. Water runs like a steady stream through her poetry, essays, and short fiction. She is currently a poetry editor for Whispering Prairie Press.

Kelly Karges is a United Methodist minister copastoring with his wife, Cindy, in Beatrice, Nebraska. They have three children, Katie, Zack, and Emily. Kelly and Cindy served churches in Charleston, South Carolina, for five years. While there, they fell in love with Folly Beach and try to return as often as possible.

Kathy Coudle King is an essayist, playwright, and novelist (*Wannabe*). She teaches writing and women's studies at the University of North Dakota, and especially enjoys facilitating writing workshops. She lives along the Red River of the North in Grand Forks, North Dakota, with her husband and four children. Contact her at *kathleen_king@und.nodak.edu* or visit her Web site: *www.angelfire.com/nd/wannabe*.

Bonnie Louise Kuchler is a writer and editor who has published nine books, including *One Heart: Universal Wisdom from the World's Scriptures*. Her series of best-selling gift books, filled with tender and funny animal pictures, includes *Just Moms*, *Just Dads*, and *Just Friends*. Bonnie's children are grown, and she lives with her husband and three Jack Russell terriers alongside a stream at the foot of the Koolau Mountains in Hawaii. Contact her at *www.bonnielouisekuchler.com*.

Virginia Lore is proud to be the mother of two preschoolers. She has had essays and articles published in *The Cohousing Journal*, *Communities Magazine*, and a number of regional Northwest publications.

Tony Luebbermann and his wife came to Tucson on their honeymoon in 1968, returned in 1969, and have lived there ever since. His longstanding interest in poetry was rekindled "by a need for spiritual and intellectual growth. To paraphrase David Whyte (*The Heart Aroused*): a need to balance the right-hand ledger of making a living with the left-hand ledger of spirituality and creativity in a new kind of double-entry bookkeeping balancing the work side of life with the life side of life." Contact him at *tonyluebbermann@earthlink.net.*

Susan Luther was born and raised in Nebraska, but long ago returned to her mother's native South. The house she shares with her husband of thirty-three years is four miles from the Tennessee River.

Margaret E. Lynch's career as an educator in religious, academic, and business settings spans more than forty years of teaching, professional writing, program development, and administration. Now living in Naples, Florida, she concentrates on creative writing in various genres. Her poetry has appeared in several anthologies, including *The Ebbing Tide, Words That Walk on the Sand,* and *Ancient Paths.* Currently, her focus is the shaping of life experiences into essay, flash fiction, and memoir.

Vivienne Mackie was born in Rhodesia (now Zimbabwe) and spent her childhood there. Later she moved to South Africa to study and work. She has always loved thunderstorms and has experienced some wild ones in many different countries. She has published a number of travel articles in magazines, newspapers, and on the Web. She now lives in the United States. Contact her at *vmackie@prairienet.org.*

James McGrath, artist, poet, and teacher, lives in Santa Fe. He is creator of the narrative poetry for the PBS *American Indian Artist Series.* He has published poetry in *Dakotah Territory, passager,* and several anthologies. He created the cover design and illustrations for *down* *wind, down diver* by William Witherup. His first poetry collection, *At the Edgelessness of Light*, was recently published.

Kathaleen McKay was born and reared in Ontario, Canada. Her passions include observing butterflies and dragonflies in nearby woodlands and exploring the snowy Lake Erie shoreline in winter. She loves the sound of rolling waves on a summer's day. Such experiences are sources of inspiration for her stories and photographic images. Kathaleen is also a proud mom. Contact her at *kaymck@sprint.ca*.

Diane Queen Miller lives in northwest Montana, follows the traditional ways of the Lakota Nation, and works with the Ikeya Wicasa (The Common People) Native American Cultural Center. She also works in radio as copywriter/producer, loves native beading and leatherwork, and dances in local powwows. Her goals in life are "to be a grandma who bakes cookies and tells stories" and "to be the voice on audio books for children and adults." Contact her at *dianequeenmiller@yahoo.com*.

Maureen Miller-Knight was raised in Fessenden, North Dakota. She received her B.B.A. and J.D. from the University of North Dakota. She has done marketing for diverse industries including student travel, advertising agency, hotel/casino, telecommunications, and electric utility, and was a college professor in Reno, Nevada. She lives in Brainerd, Minnesota, and enjoys family, travel, golf, and writing. She hopes to devote her career to writing children's books, romance, and family histories.

Tammy Murray lives in Providence, Rhode Island, and is an activities director at an independent retirement community. Her husband Tim is an executive chef. She spends her free time working toward a college degree, learning to play piano, gardening, and crocheting. Contact her at *writermom960@yahoo.com*.

Victoria Nash is a native Ohioan who steals away to the mountains of New Mexico every chance she gets. She is a freelance writer, editor, published poet, and former theater and restaurant critic. Her nonwriting hours (and there aren't many) are spent recharging her intellectual batteries by working at 84 Charing Cross, an antiquarian bookstore. This helps to feed her cat. She is currently writing a novel and finalizing a collection of poetry. Contact her at *torinash@comcast.net*.

Serena Nathan is a writer, mother of three, and wife who is lucky enough to live just a few feet from the Indian Ocean in Perth, Western Australia. Serena's writing includes internationally published short fiction and local journalism. She is currently working on her first book. Contact her at *serenan@ozemail.com.au*.

Christine O'Brien is an educator, poet, and writer. Her work has appeared in numerous publications, including *Potpourri Literary Magazine*, *Reflections*, and *Poetry Quarterly*. Much of her writing is influenced by participation in a prison ministry group at the Kansas State Penitentiary near Leavenworth. Contact her at *cmowriter@hotmail.com*.

June Owens resides in central Florida. Originally trained as a classical singer, her poems, book reviews, and nonfiction have appeared in *Atlanta Review*, *The Caribbean Writer*, *Manoa*, *Nimrod*, *Quarterly West*, *Snowy Egret*, *Spillway*, *Tirra Lirra*, and numerous anthologies. She has been the recipient of many poetry awards, among them the Prospect Press First Poetry Book Award for her collection *Tree Line*. She is also author of two prize-winning chapbooks, *Willow Moments* and *The Mask of Agamemnon*.

Bobbi Pettey is a writer, coach, and trainer. She has a communications degree and is a certified professional co-active coach. She owns Coaching Opportunities, working with people and organizations to uncover and utilize their gifts and purpose in life. She publishes *A Perspective*, a bimonthly newsletter. Bobbi lives in Minnesota with her husband, two children, and a dog. Contact her through her Web site at *www.bcoach4u.com*.

Ammini Ramachandran was born and reared in Kerala, India. After graduating with an M.A. in business and spending twenty-two years in a finance career, she is now a freelance writer researching and writing about the cuisine and culture of her home state of Kerala. She lives in New York City with her husband. Contact her at *www.peppertrail.com*.

Art Ritas taught English for thirty-three years, led interdisciplinary study tours to the Yucatan, and was codirector of the Center for Teaching and Learning at Macomb Community College. Now living in south Florida with his wife Susan, an anthropologist, he is a boat captain, master naturalist, and facilitator of creative writing workshops. He is writing a book on his kayak adventures on the Wilderness Waterway in Everglades National Park. Contact him at *ARitas540@aol.com*.

Lynn Robbins is the author and illustrator of four inspirational gift books called *Wishes…*—for women, children, men, and the broken-hearted. Her latest book, *Sit By Water*, pairs water-born poems with photographs of favorite water holes. As a freelance graphic designer, Lynn helps local poets and writers self-publish. She lives in Alexandria, Kentucky, happily near water. Contact her at *lynnrobbins@fuse.net*.

Helen M. Sadler is a graduate of Florida Gulf Coast University and is a language arts teacher. Her story "Night Music" was published in *Mangrove Review* in 2004, and her book of essays and poetry, *Turning Point*, has also been published. She lives with husband Jim and dog Macbeth in Ft. Myers, Florida, where ice never forms on her lake. Contact her at *helensadler@earthlink.net*.

Julie Ann Shapiro is a freelance writer. She won second place in Writer Online's "My First Crush Contest." Her essays and short stories have appeared in numerous publications, including *Millennium Shift*, *Story South*, *DoveTail Journal*, *Word Riot*, *Write Line*, and *Green Tricycle*. Julie is writing her second novel.

Harish C. Sharma, a native of India, is an engineer now living in Alburquerque, New Mexico. He has authored two books on environmental engineering and writes fiction, as well as nonfiction articles on a variety of subjects. His flash fiction story "Moist Oceans" won a HarMona Press award. He provides commentary on various topics for the public radio station KUNM. Contact him at *hsonai@hotmail.com*.

Deborah Shouse loves to write about the extraordinary nature of everyday life. She is a writer, speaker, editor, and creativity catalyst. Her work has appeared in *Reader's Digest, Newsweek, Woman's Day, Hemispheres, Family Circle*, and *MS*. Anthology writings include *Storming Heaven's Gate* and several *Chicken Soup* books. She has written several business books and memoirs, including *Making Your Message Memorable: Stories As Communications*. Contact her at *www.the creativityconnection.com*.

Diane Sims lives in Stratford, Ontario. Her books include *Gardens of Our Souls* (published in English, Chinese, and Japanese) and *An Ovarian Cancer Companion* (published in English and French), as well as many anthology submissions. She is accompanied in life's walk by both multiple sclerosis and ovarian cancer. Diane has adopted three feral kittens, who give her many smiles, along with the love of her life, Garth, who has reappeared to be by her side.

Harriet Smith has had many vocations and avocations: piano teacher, computer salesman, corporate executive, house painter, hotel clerk, writer. Overshadowing all was fifteen years of working as a commercial fisherman, in a small boat, usually alone. She lives in Costa Rica on the side of a volcano, raises cows and tomatoes, and continues to write. Contact her at *Hsmithcr@yahoo.com*.

Patti Tana is a professor of English at Nassau Community College (SUNY) and associate editor of the *Long Island Quarterly*. Her most recent book, *Make Your Way Across This Bridge: New & Selected Writings*, includes selections from her five earlier books and is being considered for a Pulitzer Prize. Hear Patti read "Post Humus" and other poems, and respond to them on "Connections with Patti Tana" at *www.villagenewsnet.com/connections/patti-tana.html*.

Sara Tavi is a psychologist and a writer. She lives with her husband and three children in the Boston area. She writes poetry, songs, fiction, and memoir. She enjoys writing with the Concord Writing Center and the Lighthouse Group. Contact her at *saratavi@comcast.net*.

Sharon Upp, of Laguna Niguel, California, has been a writer for over twenty years, working as national coordinator of English for *Voluntad Editorial* in Bogota, Colombia, editor of trade journals in the United States, author of an Orange County business journal astrology column, and author of poetry and vignettes. She has taught *A Course in Miracles*, served with the Alliance for Spiritual Community, and is an ordained minister of the Living Essence Foundation. Contact her at *sjmilesupp@cox.net*.

Betty Viamontes was born in Cuba and, at age fifteen, traveled to the United States as a refugee in the 1980 Mariel boatlift. She completed her undergraduate and graduate studies at the University of South Florida. She has written short stories, poems, and a memoir. Her work has appeared in *Palm Prints* 2003, *A Literary Journal of Lifelong Writers*. Contact her at *bviamont@yahoo.com*.

Melissa Wadsworth enjoyed a career in public relations for more than seventeen years. These days she is redirecting her energy to the more soul-calling endeavor of full-time writing. She recently completed her first book, a nonfiction personal growth work titled *Picture Your World! A Creative Guide to Bring Your Unique Life into Focus*. She lives in Seattle with her husband. Contact her at *wadscomm@msn.com*.

Shelley Ann Wake is a full-time author, poet, and essayist. She has degrees in science, business, and commerce, and a master of arts in professional writing. Her work has been published in various magazines, e-zines, and anthologies in Australia, Great Britain, Canada, and the United States. She is currently working on her second collection of short fiction. Contact her at *shelley_wake@yahoo.com*.

Michelle Walsh is a writer, poet, and animal rights advocate. She lives in Rhode Island, but left her heart in San Francisco. She would like to thank friends, family, and the teachings of Ram Dass for helping her though a difficult year. Michelle hopes to write a book about her life experiences. Contact her at *www.poisonedpunchbowl.com* or at *michellewalsh88@hotmail.com*.

Carole Boston Weatherford has authored numerous books of poetry, nonfiction, and children's literature, including *Sink or Swim: African-American Lifesavers of the Outer Banks; Stormy Blues; Remember the Bridge: Poems of a People*, winner of the Juvenile Literature Award from AAUW-North Carolina; and *The Sound That Jazz Makes*, winner of the Carter G. Woodson

Award and nominated for an NAACP Image Award. As a visiting distinguished professor at Fayetteville State University, she lives in High Point, North Carolina. Contact her at *weathfd@aol.com*.

Patricia Wellingham-Jones, former psychology researcher/writer/editor, has been published in journals, newspapers, and anthologies. She has won numerous awards and been featured poet in several journals.

Recent books are *Don't Turn Away: Poems About Breast Cancer*, *Labyrinth: Poems & Prose*, *Apple Blossoms at Eye Level*, and Lummox Press Little Red Book series *A Gathering Glance*. She lives in northern California. Contact her at *www.snowcrest.net/pamelaj/wellinghamjones/home.htm*.

Judith Diana Winston, visionary artist, photographer, and writer, lives in Santa Monica, California. Her book *Meditative Magic: The Pleiadean Glyphs* is in its second printing. Her forthcoming book is *The Keeper of the Diary*. Her photo series, *Dolphins I Have Known*, is a tribute to her watery friends. She sees her work as a marriage of her creativity with her spiritual journey. She is a lover of all things wild. Contact her at *j.ddolphin@verizon.net*.

Anthony Woodlief is president of the Mercatus Center at George Mason University, an organization devoted to research, education, and outreach. He has published short fiction in the Webzines *Banshee Studios* and *Doorknobs and Bodypaint*, and is completing a novel. More of his writing can be found at *www.tonywoodlief.com*. Anthony lives in Virginia with his wife and three sons.

Cherise Wyneken is retired from teaching and raising four children. She lives with her husband in Albany, California, and has enjoyed sharing her prose and poetry with readers through a variety of journals, periodicals, and anthologies. She has published two books of poetry, *Touchstones* and *Seeded Puffs*, and *Round Trip*, a memoir that depicts her spiritual journey. Contact her at *cwyneken@sbcglobal.net*.

Ron Yeomans is a semiretired gynecologist, part-time fisherman, and more or less full-time spiritual seeker who occasionally, in moments of weakness, commits some of his thoughts and memories to paper.

To My Readers

If you have a comment, question, or story to share, or
would like to be on my newsletter mailing list, please
contact me at *www.sacredfeathers.com* or send a letter (with
a self-addressed, stamped envelope for a reply) to:

Maril Crabtree
6045 Martway Ste. 104
Mission, KS 66202

Please check my Web site for workshops, readings, or
other events in your area. I appreciate hearing from you!